Cultural Conflicts

Case Studies in a World of Change

Edward Lerner

J. WESTON
WALCH
PUBLISHER

PORTLAND, MAINE

User's Guide
to
Walch Reproducible Books

As part of our general effort to provide educational materials which are as practical and economical as possible, we have designated this publication a "reproducible book." The designation means that purchase of the book includes purchase of the right to limited reproduction of all pages on which this symbol appears:

Here is the basic Walch policy: We grant to individual purchasers of this book the right to make sufficient copies of reproducible pages for use by all students of a single teacher. This permission is limited to a single teacher, and does not apply to entire schools or school systems, so institutions purchasing the book should pass the permission on to a single teacher. Copying of the book or its parts for resale is prohibited.

Any questions regarding this policy or requests to purchase further reproduction rights should be addressed to:

Permissions Editor
J. Weston Walch, Publisher
321 Valley Street • P. O. Box 658
Portland, Maine 04104-0658

Cover Photo: © Alain Le Garsmeur/Tony Stone Worldwide
Workers' houses in Fushua, Liaoning Province, China

1   2   3   4   5   6   7   8   9   10
ISBN 0-8251-2605-3

Contents

Foreword to the Revised Edition

When this book was originally published in 1986, its goal was to help prepare students to understand some of the issues involved in the rapid cultural changes of our time. Reader responses have indicated that the book was indeed useful in pursuing that goal. However, that very purpose created a special concern: If we included really urgent cultural conflicts, some of them were likely to produce changes that would render particular case studies obsolete in a few years.

For example, the original edition explored tensions created in the Soviet Union by the search for a national identity by people in the Baltic republics. In the ensuing years, that conflict led to the total withdrawal by those republics from the Soviet Union and its successor, the Commonwealth of Independent States. On the other hand, the case study on Western Europe looked at the status of Turkish immigrant workers in Germany—a conflict that is now, if anything, even more urgent, yet unresolved.

Accordingly, this edition reflects changes in the world and in commentary since 1986. Where change has already taken place, as in the former Soviet Union, the case has been replaced. Where the original conflict is still ongoing, the case selection has been retained in updated form.

Because so much still rests upon the foundation of the original book, we are reprinting here the Foreword to the original edition.

Foreword to the Original Edition

This book came about through a combination of classroom experiences and discussions with fellow educators. However, the direct inspiration was my experience in helping Americans understand some of the complexities of the culture of the Druze people.

I was privileged to spend some time in that remarkable Arab community during the summer of 1983, when I was a Fulbright Fellow in Israel. Continuing dialogues with members of the Druze community led directly to the identification of this book's key concepts. I would therefore like particularly to acknowledge the assistance of Jamal Yusuf Ali of Pikiin, Riyad Felah of Kafr Sumiya, and Druze friends in the Galilee, who helped me understand some of the issues involved in the conflict between modernization and traditional societies.

I would like specifically to acknowledge as inspiration for the entire project Mr. Arie Shoval, deputy director general of the Ministry of Education and Culture of the State of Israel. His work for the Fulbright program and many other ventures has immeasurably advanced the cause of international understanding.

Especially helpful on particular topics were Dr. Bessie Lyman of the Newton public schools for her personal observations of Zimbabwe, Mr. John Bendix of Indiana University for his studies of guest workers in West Germany, Ms. Leslie Swartz and Ms. Leslie Bedford of the Harvard East Asian Program for their observations on China and Japan respectively, and, for many helpful suggestions, two colleagues in the Harvard Outreach Program, Mrs. Catherine Jones of the Center for Middle Eastern Studies and Dr. Janet Vaillant of the Soviet and East European Language and Culture Center. A number of Newton teachers and students were also quite helpful in testing and critiquing classroom materials. Mrs. Ann Nicoletta did most of the basic manuscript typing.

The most important support came from my wife, Joan Bryan Lerner, and our daughters, Elizabeth and Jennifer. They have contributed in more ways than can be counted.

Introduction

In our increasingly interdependent world, students have become familiar with information about other cultures around the globe. They are also aware of the constant change taking place in many parts of this world. However, many students lack a sense of the complexity of social change. They have difficulty with questions like these: Is modernization inevitable in traditional societies? What changes are being considered in various cultures? Are changes "good" for everyone? What factors promote change? What factors resist change?

Accordingly, this book presents a series of cultural change situations around the world. Each case concerns an issue that is particularly vital in its culture today. Fictitious characters are given representative positions that highlight the major responses to the issue in the special context of a particular culture. By acting out these roles and engaging in efforts to persuade each other, students come to see the human dimensions of major issues.

However, the cases are not parochial ones; the issues are important in other cultures besides the society under study. Students are therefore presented opportunities for both analyzing the special attributes of a culture and exploring an issue that is significant for many cultures.

Recommended Teacher Readings

Anthropology Curriculum Study Project. *Modernization and Traditional Societies.* New York: Macmillan, 1971.

Black, C.E. *The Dynamics of Modernization.* New York: Harper and Row, 1967.

Brislin, Richard W. *Cross-Cultural Encounters.* New York: Pergamon Press, 1981.

Chapman, Katherine, James E. Davis, and Andrea Meier. *Simulation Games in the Social Studies: What Do We Know?* Boulder, CO: Social Science Education Consortium, 1979.

Fersh, Seymour. *Learning About People and Cultures.* Evanston, IL: McDougal Littell, 1974.

Harvey, Robert G. *An Attainable Global Perspective.* New York: Global Perspectives, 1979.

Lamy, Steven, Roger Myers, Debbie Von Vihl, and Katherine Weeks. *Teaching Global Awareness with Simulations and Games.* Denver: University of Denver, 1983.

Mehlinger, Howard. *Global Studies for American Schools.* Washington, DC: National Education Association, 1979.

Smith, Gary R., and George Otero. *Teaching About Cultural Awareness.* Denver: CTIR, University of Denver, 1977.

Switzer, Kenneth, and Paul Mulloy. *Global Issues: Activities and Resources for the High School Teacher.* Denver: CTIR, University of Denver, 1979.

World Bank Staff. *Toward a Better World: The Developing World.* Washington, DC: The World Bank, 1983.

How to Use the Cases

Each case consists of four parts:

1. A background section (including a reproducible map), to alert the teacher to the themes, provide special information about the culture, and suggest opportunities to apply the theme to other cultures.

2. A scenario, to explain the specific situation being presented in the simulation.

3. A set of individual roles, for which students will prepare their presentations.

4. A bibliography, presenting current resources for teacher and student use in further exploring the issue and the culture.

Suggested Teaching Sequence

1. Read the background section. You may want to share some of this with your class, depending on how much previous study of the culture they have done and what other materials are in use.

2. Make copies of the scenario, and distribute one to each student. Use a class session to make sure the information is clearly understood.

3. Make copies of the roles and assign them to specific students. There are a minimum of ten roles per case. For large classes, you may give the same role to two or more students. (Some teachers prefer to change the name when giving an identical role to another student.) You should decide whether each student's preparation of a simulated role should consist of speaking notes or a full written statement of position.

4. Projects on the culture under discussion can be presented via writing, drawing, music, dance, etc. Topics can include history, religion, traditions, and people of that culture in America.

5. Students can adapt the same issue for a different culture. For example, if the class has just done the case study on urbanization in Latin America, students can create roles on this topic set in another culture

they have studied—for instance, Southeast Asia. Their work should demonstrate understanding of the issue and of the nature of Southeast Asia.

6. Students can do research reports on the actual topic of a case study—e.g., details on the Francophone movement in Quebec—or an aspect of the culture in the case—e.g., how independence was achieved in Zimbabwe.

7. The class can create its own simulation of a cultural conflict within another society. The nature of the curriculum and the particular class can determine how closely to follow a case study in this book—e.g., whether to use a situation focused on a young woman in a nontraditional role—and how much detail about the particular culture should be researched. The arguments worked out for the newly created characters can demonstrate how well students have understood issues involved in dealing with cultural conflicts in changing societies.

Case Studies

Culture Area	Issue
Japan	Individualism Versus Corporate Life
China	Choices: Economic Freedom Without Civil Liberties
India	Maintaining the Caste System
Southeast Asia	Extended or Nuclear Family Living?
Russia and the Commonwealth of Independent States	Guiding Principles in a Time of Transition
Western Europe	The Role of Foreign Workers
North Africa and the Middle East	Women's Roles in a Traditional Society
Africa South of the Sahara	Nationalism Versus Tribal Loyalties
South America	Urbanization Versus Village Life
Central America	Reform or Revolution?
Canada	A National or Local Language?
United States of America	Multiculturalism and National Unity

JAPAN

Individualism Versus Corporate Life

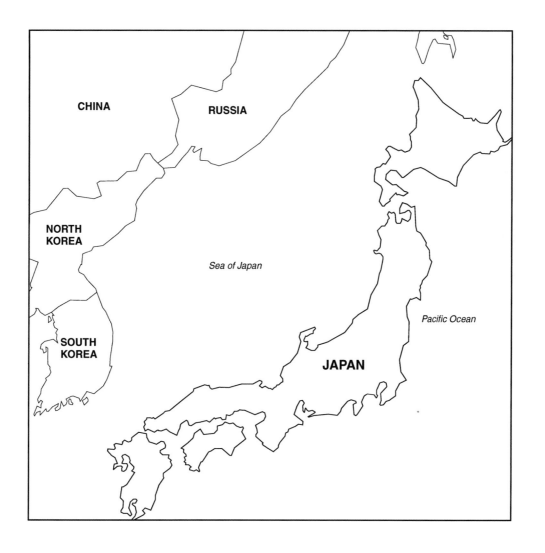

CHINA

RUSSIA

NORTH KOREA

Sea of Japan

SOUTH KOREA

Pacific Ocean

JAPAN

BACKGROUND

The spectacular achievements of Japan's "company system" and the distinctive personal life it creates have captured the interest of many writers, particularly Americans. The search for explanations of Japanese industrial performance in competition with the United States has led us to examine and evaluate Japanese methods. This simulation presents a Japanese man evaluating the system's impact upon himself. To present a viewpoint that is easier for our students to handle, the Japanese protagonist has been given exposure to American values against which to measure his own experiences. With the increased involvement of Japanese experts in their companies' activities in the United States, this is not unrealistic.

Some of the specifics offered in the simulation—e.g., the daily performance of the company song by the assembled employees of Matsushita—may be hard for American students to accept. You might, therefore, want to show one of the number of educational videos on contemporary Japan that include such sequences. Two possibilities are: *Two Factories: Japan and America*, LCA Films, 1974, 22 minutes; *The Human Face of Japan: Lifetime Employment*, LCA Films, 1982, 28 minutes.

Although few industrialized societies have attempted to copy the Japanese company system, it might be interesting to consider the system's potential. Students might discuss whether some aspects of the Japanese model would be useful for American application.

SCENARIO

Hiroshi Tashino is a computer engineer for the Fujitsu Corporation, a major Japanese manufacturer of computer equipment. He has been working for the company for fifteen years, ever since his graduation from Tokyo University. He and his wife now have two children. His career has been quite successful, and he has had a number of promotions.

He has recently returned to Japan from a year in the United States, where he was in Fujitsu's California office. While in the United States, he thought up a new system for creating computer programs.

Hiroshi has tried to interest his company in his new idea but has been turned down. He still believes it is a good concept; he is thinking of leaving Fujitsu and starting his own small company to implement his ideas.

Because company loyalty is very strong in Japan, Hiroshi wants to talk to friends and relatives before making his decision.

HIROSHI TASHINO

Although you had not been especially unhappy with Fujitsu, you now are interested in going out on your own. You were very impressed by the booming electronics companies you saw in California's "Silicon Valley"—the center of the computer research industry—that had been started by engineers who left big corporations.

Fujitsu's decision to turn down your proposal was a great disappointment. In traditional fashion, a number of company officials met with you to try to convince you that your concept would not fit well into the company's plans. They assumed you were still committed to what is best for the corporation.

You do feel gratitude to the company for all its support. Your life has been heavily involved with Fujitsu. It has arranged the financing of your house, and its employees are the people involved in nearly all of your social life.

Leaving would be quite difficult but also exciting.

KIMIKO TASHINO

You are Hiroshi's wife. You have accepted the traditional role of a Japanese wife and have become involved in activities organized by the Fujitsu Corporation. You have attended classes in flower arranging and Japanese ceremonies taught by Fujitsu teachers. Most of your social events have been company-sponsored.

In California, you were particularly influenced by new friends who were Japanese-Americans. Those women picked their own activities, even though some of their husbands worked for big American computer corporations. They kept their family lives separate from their husbands' and their own employers.

That period of privacy—when everyone did not know everything you did—was enjoyable. Perhaps you can have that in Japan if Hiroshi starts his own small company.

You will suggest to Hiroshi that he leave Fujitsu.

SABURO MATSUOKA

You are an engineer at the Fujitsu Corporation. You work in the same department as Hiroshi Tashino, and the two of you are friends. He has told you he might leave the company, and you are concerned.

You think it would be a mistake to leave, although you know that many people have tried their own enterprises. Recently, nearly 100,000 small companies were started by people leaving big businesses and trying to make it on their own. Most of these companies were involved in high-technology fields like computer programming.

But these small enterprises are very risky. Many fail, and none of them can guarantee the kind of lifetime security the great corporations have provided so well. A man like Hiroshi, with a wife and two children to support, should stay with the proven security of Fujitsu.

You will discourage him from taking such a risk.

AKIRA TASHINO

You are Hiroshi's older brother. Since you do not have his academic talent, you did not go to a university. But you did get a good technical education. You work in the quality control department of the Matsushita Electric Corporation, which makes Panasonic appliances.

You are quite happy with your job at the huge Matsushita plant near Osaka. You live in a company apartment house. You even married your wife in the chapel at the company recreation center. The togetherness of employees is something you really enjoy.

The spirit of teamwork has been well developed at Matsushita, and you think it is the key reason for the company's success. In your quality control job, you seldom find production errors. The employees' sense of team responsibility makes their work more careful.

You believe that Fujitsu has created similar team feelings for Hiroshi, and you think it would be a mistake for him to abandon them. You will tell him so.

ICHIRO TASHINO

You are Hiroshi's younger brother. When you were looking for a job, you followed the advice of your oldest brother, Akira. You joined his employer, Matsushita Electric, the company that makes Panasonic products.

As Akira promised, Matsushita supplied all of your basic needs, from a company supermarket to a company apartment house. You were delighted to have all this taken care of for you.

But that was some years ago. Now you are changing your mind. The company apartment house is cheaper than other housing, but it means you are surrounded by your co-workers at home as well as on the job. The company recreation program means that you spend your play time with the same people you work with. Your life seems very limited.

You will encourage Hiroshi to start his own company. You might even ask him if you could join him there.

ETSUKO TASHINO

You are Hiroshi's sister-in-law. Your husband, Akira, has worked for a big business, the Matsushita Electric Corporation, for many years. Now that your children are older, you have also gone to work for Matsushita.

You are quite happy with the company. You are proud of the worldwide success of the Panasonic brand appliances you work on at Matsushita. It is invigorating to start each work day with your fellow employees, dressed in identical blue uniforms, as you join in singing the company song. In music, you praise the company's growth. That spirit of togetherness—of being part of a successful team—is important.

The achievements of the great Japanese corporations have earned the admiration of the world. You take special pride in noticing the groups of visitors from the United States and Europe. They come to your factory to try to understand the cause of Panasonic's accomplishments.

You know that if Hiroshi starts his own business, he will lose all these good feelings. He will soon be unhappy, and his family life will then suffer.

You will suggest that Hiroshi stay with the proven ways of the past.

PATRICK MORINAGA

You are a Japanese-American from San Jose, California. You knew Hiroshi and Kimiko Tashino when they lived in the United States. Now you are visiting Japan and have come to see the Tashinos.

You are happy to hear that Hiroshi is interested in starting his own company. You always considered him unusually intelligent and creative. You suspected that his talents may have been somewhat held back by all the emphasis on group thinking and planning in Japanese corporations.

You have done very well with your own small company in California. You know a number of computer engineers who have also done well on their own. There is a constant need to make quick innovations in computer programs. This means there will always be opportunities for small companies that can go quickly from ideas to completion. Hiroshi seems well trained to do that.

You will urge Hiroshi to start out on his own. You may even suggest special arrangements with your own company.

OHISA KAGUCHI

You are Hiroshi's younger sister. You teach English at a middle school, but you are well informed about the computer industry in your country. Hiroshi's wife, Kimiko, has told you about his interest in starting his own business.

It sounds like a good idea to you. You and your husband are both teachers, and your lives are quite different from those of Hiroshi and his family. You have much more independence in what you do at home. You do not need to participate in company housing, company recreation, or company clubs. You choose for yourselves what you want to do. No one wonders why you are not doing what others in the same office are doing.

You still take a lot of interest in your work. In fact, a lot of your time is spent keeping in touch with former students as well as handling the work of your classes. But your social life is your own. Sometimes you spend time with teachers. At other times, you relax with friends and neighbors who have nothing to do with schools.

You think your brother and sister-in-law would enjoy a more private life also. You will suggest that Hiroshi leave the corporation.

HIDEKI YOSAWA

You are a retired mathematics teacher. Hiroshi Tashino was one of your favorite students, and you have kept in touch over the years. Hiroshi has written to you about his idea of leaving Fujitsu for his own company.

You are not sure what advice to give him. You know that many small companies have been created in the field of computer programming. Some of them are doing well. But you want to be sure that Hiroshi would not leave Fujitsu for the wrong reasons.

You are proud of Japanese traditions and of the great achievements of Japanese companies in the markets of the world. You think it is especially important that the great corporations have given a distinctly Japanese character to their way of operating. All of the copying of American and European styles in clothing, music, and food has upset you. No American company would have its workers dress identically and sing company songs. Therefore, that is a special reason for Japanese companies to do so.

You will tell Hiroshi it is important to maintain the special Japanese way of running a company. He should not challenge those customs.

YOSHIDA DAKAI

You are a long-time friend of Hiroshi. You went to high school and college together. However, the two of you have not been together as often as you would like, because most of Hiroshi's socializing is done with people from his company.

You understand that this pattern is necessary and is typical of people who work for large companies. That is an important reason for your wanting Hiroshi to start his own business. Then his private life would be more flexible.

You can remind him of how much of his private life—from company-supplied baby-sitters to company-arranged vacation trips—has been decided for him by his employers. You know it is not his fault that he has little time for old friends. Still, you feel he could change this situation by changing jobs.

You will urge him to start his own business and get control of his personal as well as his professional activities.

BIBLIOGRAPHY

Bernson, Mary H., and Betsy Goolian, eds. *Modern Japan: An Idea Book for K-12 Teachers.* Bloomington, IN: The National Clearinghouse for United States–Japan Studies, 1992.

Cogan, John, and Donald O. Schneider, eds. *Perspectives on Japan: A Guide for Teachers.* Washington, DC: NCSS, 1983.

Dolan, Edward F., and Shan Finney. *The New Japan.* New York: Franklin Watts, 1983.

Fairbank, John K., Edwin O. Reischauer, and Albert M. Craig. *East Asia: Tradition and Transformation.* Boston: Houghton Mifflin, 1978.

Kawatama, Kazuhide. *We Live in Japan.* New York: Bookwright Press, 1984.

Laver, Ross, and Masako Shimizu. "The Company Man." Toronto: *Maclean's,* November 1991.

Lebra, Takie. *Japanese Patterns of Behavior.* Honolulu: University of Hawaii Press, 1984.

Minear, Richard, ed. *Through Japanese Eyes: The Present.* New York: Praeger, 1991.

Reischauer, Edwin O. *Japan.* New York: Knopf, 1981.

Shirey, Donald. *Tradition and Modernization in Japanese Culture.* Princeton: Princeton University Press, 1971.

Vogel, Ezra F. *Japan as Number One.* New York: Harper and Row, 1980.

CHINA

Choices: Economic Freedom Without Civil Liberties

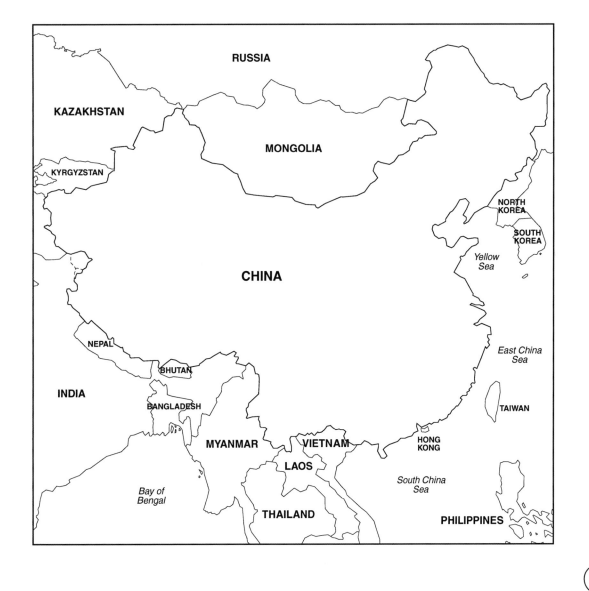

BACKGROUND

This simulation deals with a general theme—whether individual freedom can be presented in the economic arena without being allowed in the political arena—but the issues are presented in a way that is reflective of the special history of recent China. Students should be aware of the democracy movement of 1989 and the harsh repression it received, as well as the current unleashing of capitalist impulses and the impressive economic growth that has resulted.

The overall tension between economic freedom and political repression is an issue in many Third World societies seeking the key to upgrading their economies. In this simulation, other issues—for example, the threat of capitalism to the philosophical base of a Communist society—are interwoven with the general theme.

The question of risk-taking—whether to totally commit oneself to a way of life that had been officially forbidden for two generations—has been a concern in times of unpredictable change. Students do not have to know many particulars of a society to visualize the doubts that might assail an ambitious individual in troubled times. Indeed, some of the best source material could be Shakespeare's characters.

Although China has spent most of the twentieth century in various stages of revolution, it still has a powerful Confucian tradition. It is therefore important for students to realize that advice from relatives is not treated just as it would be in America. Young people in China seem to be drawing back toward family influence, as respect for the old revolutionary doctrines fades and deeper values return. Similar patterns are important in most cultures.

SCENARIO

Ling Buzhong is in his final year of study at Beijing Qinghua University, a famous school devoted to engineering. He has done well in his engineering classes and is popular among his fellow students.

Although he has not been involved in many activities outside classes, he has friends who have talked a lot about political change. They have suggested that he accept a scholarship he has been offered at the University of California at Berkeley, and use that opportunity to organize criticism of the government from the safety of the United States.

Other classmates are less politically minded and propose that a group of them use their engineering ability to set up a new high technology company. One classmate has already contacted some people in Hong Kong who might put up the money to start the company, but the Hong Kong investors especially want Ling, Qinghua's top student in this field, to be part of the company.

Now he is on vacation and is visiting his family in a town near Beijing. His father, Ling Moshu, has arranged a party of close friends and relatives. The purpose is to see Ling Buzhong and to offer him useful advice.

The friends and relatives include people who have been involved in some of the major events of Chinese life in the past twenty years. Their experiences through that period often influence their opinions. Ling Buzhong knows that some of these people have suffered badly in the past and are sincerely interested in helping him avoid similar misfortunes. Others have done well and have their own ideas about success. They also want to share their ideas with him.

Ling Buzhong will have to decide which advice, if any, to follow.

LING BUZHONG

You are about to complete your studies at Beijing Qinghua University. You are the top student in your field, and people have tried to recruit you for the new private companies that are springing up. In fact, a group of your friends has received an offer from Hong Kong investors to create a new company, if you will agree to be on its staff.

You have also been offered a scholarship to do advanced studies at the University of California at Berkeley. Some of the world's most advanced research is being done there, and you understand that the university has a large group of Chinese and Chinese-American students. Other friends suggest that if you go to Berkeley you could stay there after your program is completed, continue to do research, and use it as a base to publish criticism of the lack of political freedom in China.

Your understanding of English is quite good, and you are confident that you could succeed at either the business venture or the study program in America. You also know that your reputation among Chinese students and scholars would cause them to pay attention to anything you might write from America. You have been aware that people who want to rise in China cannot be politically active, but you were very upset by the government's brutal tactics in crushing the democracy movement. You are aware of how carefully police agents keep track of any possible criticism of the government.

You are also aware of your responsibility to your family. They have supported you as a student, and they are now expecting you to do something to bring honor and personal benefits to them.

LING MOSHU

You were trained as an engineer yourself and are very proud that your son has entered the same field, although at a much more advanced level. But you hope that your son will not experience the same difficulties you did.

You were educated in the United States, graduating from the Massachusetts Institute of Technology in 1950. The Communists had then just completed their victory in the Civil War. They announced that they were offering special opportunities to Chinese who had received specialized training overseas and would come home to help rebuild the nation. You accepted the offer and were given important responsibilities in some major projects.

In 1965 you were arrested during the Great Cultural Revolution. People with American or European training were considered suspicious. You lost your engineering job and had to spend 10 years as a cement carrier. In 1977 you were restored to an engineering position.

You feel that your own background made you stand out among people who all had training and backgrounds similar to each other. You are therefore worried that either the new business project or the advanced study in California would set your son apart from others. In a society where the government has emphasized conformity and has the power to punish people for things that were actually encouraged at the time they happened, it may be wisest to do only what everyone else does.

You want to warn Ling Buzhong to turn down both offers and take a safe position in a government-sponsored program.

PANG WEI

You are a female student at Beijing Qinghua University. You have some classes with Ling Buzhong, and you know that he is both a gifted engineer and a natural leader. You think he is the kind of person who could revive the movement toward democracy that was crushed by the government in 1989.

At the same time, the most advanced research in new engineering is being done in the United States. Someone who could be trained there could one day become one of China's foremost engineers.

You know that China's leaders want to establish closer trade relations with the United States; they would be very careful about harassing a Chinese who was known and active in that country. They might take seriously criticisms that came from an American-based scientist who had no previous reputation as an opponent of the regime.

You will try to persuade Ling Buzhong to take the California offer, and use it to both improve his own training and issue calls for political freedom in China.

BAI KENG

You are a high school teacher. Ling Buzhong was your best student, and you are delighted to see how well he has done at Beijing Qinghua University. Although your own subject is history, you feel that engineering is important for the future of your country.

It has always upset you that China has much less power in the world than its size and population deserve. You feel that the limited power is tied to the limited level of Chinese technology. You want China to do whatever is necessary to advance its technology.

Clearly, the most advanced technology is found in the United States, Western Europe, and Japan. It is therefore necessary for people involved in technological fields like engineering to get all they can from those foreign countries. Then China can take its rightful place in the world.

You have heard that Ling Buzhong may also be interested in political reform, but you feel that it is not for you to raise that topic. You will simply try to convince him to study in California.

WANG QI

You are an aunt of Ling Buzhong. You are a health official, and all of your own training has been in China. You have seen that Chinese medical education was set back very badly by the Cultural Revolution, which downgraded and punished people with foreign training. As a result, China is far behind in many areas of modern medical practice.

It is clear to you that China needs modernization, and modernization cannot be achieved without Western technology. Your nephew looks like exactly the kind of person who could both benefit personally from foreign training and make good use of it to benefit China.

You are also aware of both the recent democracy movement and the terrible price that was paid by those students who led it in 1989. You hope that a new generation of political leaders will take over and sponsor freedom, but you think that people should not now risk themselves in a hopeless struggle for more rights. You think that Ling Buzhong should stay out of politics.

You want to persuade your nephew to do advanced studies in California, but drop any connection with political movements.

LING ZHIYUAN

You are an elder cousin of Ling Buzhong. You are unhappy with the way things seem to be going lately in China. When you were still a boy, you fought in the Red Army that won the Civil War to bring communism to China. Now you wonder what has become of your country.

You feel that too many people have forgotten that the whole purpose of China's revolution was to make the country into a Communist society. Now people talk openly of getting richer than their neighbors, and the government seems to be encouraging foreign capitalist investments. And here is your own cousin thinking about an offer to help start a profit-making business on behalf of a group of investors from Hong Kong—the city whose people chose capitalism over communism.

You feel that your cousin should neither go to study in capitalist America nor help bring more capitalism to China. He should stay here and work for one of the state-run Communist industries.

CHEN XILEN

You are a female student at Beijing Qinghua University. You are one of the group that is hoping to be among the engineers at the new company that Ling Buzhong's friends are proposing. Female engineers are relatively new in China, and this could be a great opportunity for you.

You also believe that the new company would be a good thing for the Chinese people. You are sure that many of China's problems today come from the years when your country was dominated by Europe, the United States, and Japan. For Ling Buzhong to go to one of those countries for additional training, instead of immediately helping to build Chinese industries, would be unfaithful to the brave heroes who threw the foreigners out of China.

China will never be a truly independent nation as long as Chinese engineers have to depend on foreign experts for training. You want Ling Buzhong to see and accept that important idea.

LING WEI

You are Ling Buzhong's mother. You are very happy that he has done so well at engineering school and has been given a choice of offers. He has told you about the idea of starting up the new business; that sounds like the best choice.

You have known real poverty, especially during the years of the Cultural Revolution, when your husband had his job taken away. You learned two lessons from that experience: get ahold of a lot of money to carry you through any economic setback, and be alert to changes in the official policies. That way you can take advantage of opportunities and not get caught being too far ahead of what is tolerated.

It is therefore clear to you that your son should join the new company. The government seems to approve, and after all it will bring new jobs and higher technology to China. At the same time, he should drop any contacts with people who demand more political freedom. That will only get him into trouble and destroy his chance for a great future. You are also counting on your son's success to support the whole family, including your own retirement years.

You will try to persuade Ling Buzhong to join the businessmen and drop all politics.

DENG TUNG

You are Ling Buzhong's classmate at Beijing Qinghua University. You have worked on a number of projects with him and find that, together with some other classmates, you make a powerful and effective team. When some Hong Kong relatives said that they knew people who were interested in organizing a new high-technology company in China using young Chinese engineers, you set up the arrangements. But the businessmen made it clear that the key to the venture would be Ling Buzhong, known as the most brilliant engineering student at the university.

China seems to be on the verge of explosive economic growth. The method is open capitalism, even though the government remains officially Communist. If you can get in on the ground floor, when new companies are just starting, there are fortunes to be made. Your specific proposal looks especially good, because it has Hong Kong backers; when Hong Kong is reunited with China in a few years, your company will be in a great position to take advantage of the opportunities that will result.

All of the students' families have made sacrifices to educate them; getting rich will repay them as well as benefit yourselves. Let others worry about political issues; you want to live well. Now you have to sell Ling Buzhong on that idea.

KIANG HSU

You are a longtime friend of Ling Buzhong. Although you went to a teacher's college while he went into engineering, you have maintained the friendship that began in childhood. Now you are among those who secretly plan ways to restart the movement toward democracy that was suppressed a few years ago. Ling Buzhong knows this, and you have discussed it together.

Although you understand that he will gain important advanced training in California, you think political goals are an even more important reason for him to go there. It has been very difficult to stay connected to the pro-democracy Chinese who have gone to America and dare not return, but Ling Buzhong could get in touch with them once there. He could also recruit support for your movement among the Chinese-American community. That might influence the Chinese government to become liberal enough to allow Ling Buzhong to return as both a highly trained engineer and a spokesman for democracy.

You intend to try to convince him to go to America to work for Chinese democracy.

BIBLIOGRAPHY

Benegar, John, et al. *Changing Images of China*. Denver: Center for Teaching International Relations, 1983.

Bernstein, Richard. *From the Center of the Earth*. Boston: Little Brown, 1982.

Butterfield, Fox. *China: Alive in the Bitter Sea*. New York: Times Books, 1982.

Fersh, Seymour. *Asia: Teaching About/ Learning From*. New York, Teachers College Press, 1977.

Gargan, Edward. *China's Fate: A People's Turbulent Struggle with Reform and Repression*. New York: Doubleday, 1990.

Hsu, Immanuel. *The Rise of Modern China*. New York: Oxford University Press, 1983.

Human Rights in China, Inc. *Children of the Dragon*. New York: Collier Books, 1990.

Kalat, Marie B., and Elizabeth Hoermann. *China Connections*. Boston: Community Learning Connections, 1988.

Martin, Roberta, et al. *Contemporary China: A Teaching Workbook*. New York: East Asia Curriculum Project of Columbia University, 1990.

Seybolt, Peter, ed. *Through Chinese Eyes*. New York: Praeger, 1991.

Terrill, Ross. "China's Youth Wait for Tomorrow." *National Geographic*, July 1991.

Thompson, Carol, ed. *The People's Republic of China*. Philadelphia: Current History, 1992.

INDIA

Maintaining the Caste System

BACKGROUND

The caste system was officially abolished when India gained independence and created a new constitution. Nevertheless, many of the rules of the caste system continued to be maintained, particularly in the villages. Even Mahatma Gandhi's efforts to end restrictions on the lowest—or untouchable—caste had little impact. In 1955 the Untouchability Offenses Act made it illegal to enforce untouchability by social or economic boycott, but the act has been poorly enforced. Caste restrictions are so deeply rooted that their disappearance is not expected in the near future.

In simulating a discussion of the caste system by people involved in it, it is important to have students realize that it is not simply a system of exploitation imposed on weaker people by powerful ones. There are many people on the lower end of the caste system who seem to accept readily what appear to us to be oppressive limitations.

Another factor in Indian attitudes has not been explored in this case study: the role of religious belief. Hinduism, with its concepts of karma, dharma, and reincarnation, can be a major influence on one's attitude toward caste. However, we have set up the simulation so it can be used by students without special understanding of Hindu religious beliefs.

In thinking about wider implications of abandoning a caste identity, students can consider situations where a person is permanently identified in a particular way in a community and feels that the only way to be considered for other roles is to leave town permanently. What would go into such a decision?

SCENARIO

Krishnan Rojatli is a sandalmaker's son in a village in India. A terrible flood has occurred in the mountains, and Krishnan is among the young men who volunteered to go there and build emergency flood barriers. Their work was successful, and Krishnan has recently returned to the village.

Gapur Rojatli is Krishnan's father. He is a widely respected sandalmaker. Everyone expects him eventually to pass his shop and customers on to his sons. Gapur has always accepted the fact that in India all trades associated with animal hides and skins, like sandalmaking, are considered low caste. They are appropriate only for his own low caste.

Krishnan, on the other hand, has been dramatically changed by his experiences in the flood control project. For the first time, he has spent a sustained period living and working among people from many villages and many castes. During the project they worked as equals, under the leadership of an army officer who did not care for the caste system. Krishnan found this an exciting experience, and it has led him to question his family's caste tradition. He is therefore thinking about leaving the village and dropping out of the caste system.

KRISHNAN ROJATLI

You are 30 years old. You and your brothers work in the family's sandal-making shop. Although there are no other sandalmakers in the village, there is really not enough income from the shop to provide a decent living for the many members of your family. But sandalmaking is the traditional activity of your subcaste. That expectation has never been questioned by anyone in the village.

Your experiences in the flood control emergency team have excited you about the idea of starting a new life without the limitations of caste. You realize that this would not be possible in your village without making problems for your parents and others. So you think you should leave the village and take your family to some big city.

GAPUR ROJATLI

You have been a sandalmaker in the village all your life, and you inherited your shop from your own father. It is very difficult to support all your family from the one business. Nevertheless, you take pride in the fact that your sons will carry on the family tradition.

The caste system does not seem a problem to you; everyone knows exactly where he or she fits in. You are happy you don't have to learn all the complicated ceremonies that upper-caste Brahmins have to know. You wouldn't want to have to be careful to avoid touching animal products as Brahmins do.

You don't understand why your son does not accept this. You have to convince him to stay with the old ways.

SANTHA ROJATLI

You are 28 years old and are the wife of Krishnan. Your own family is from the same caste as your husband, but from a different village. You were very poor; it was hard for your parents to raise the money for your dowry when you got married. But everyone felt it was a good choice to be married to a responsible man like Krishnan.

You have never traveled outside your own or your husband's village. You have heard that life is different in the cities and that the caste system is not strictly followed there. You are nervous about the idea of living without caste traditions.

You feel that your marriage is successful because you and your husband came from the same caste. You knew when you married what food, customs, and ideas your husband would like—those of the caste. Living without caste traditions would be frightening, but you could not oppose your husband's decision.

MANTU SINGH

You are an officer in the Indian Army. You are a Sikh, not a Hindu, so your religion does not put you into the caste system. When you were in the flood control project, you were impressed by the intelligence and hard work of the village men who labored for you. You would like to help them.

Krishnan Rojatli seems exactly the kind of person who could get ahead by leaving his village. He is interested in new ideas and the possibility of changing lifelong traditions.

You feel that such thinking would make it easier to adopt the kind of modern innovations that could solve India's problems. For example, the terrible flood might have been avoided if villagers were willing to change the dangerous but traditional ways that the river waters have always been channeled.

You want to encourage Krishnan to leave his village and his caste and to start a new life elsewhere.

ARUNA ROJATLI

You are Krishnan's younger sister. You are 15 years old; the family will soon be arranging for your engagement. Because the Rojatli family is so poor, you will not have a very good choice of husbands. You fear that you will be sent to some very poor man in another village in the remote mountains.

You have asked Krishnan about the possibility of your going to the city with his family. If he does move there, you want to go with him. You would take your chances on a better marriage opportunity than you could get in the village.

You will try to convince Krishnan to move as soon as possible.

SUDHIR ROJATLI

You are Krishnan's older brother and are also a sandalmaker in your father's shop. You have always lived in the village and are comfortable with the traditional way of life. You don't know whether there really are more opportunities in the cities. Even if there were, you would not want to change your life to try them.

Your own wife and children seem happy with their existence among fellow members of your caste. They would probably be nervous trying to fit in among really different people in a strange place. So it does not seem to make sense for you to consider moving.

You like your brother Krishnan and enjoy working together in the shop. If he goes, he would be making a bad decision, and you would be losing the company of a brother at work and play.

You will try to persuade him to stay.

Arjun Rojatli

You are Krishnan's younger brother. You are still single and are also still learning the craft of sandalmaking. But with a small shop to support so many relatives, you know you will always be very poor. Although you are not ready to leave your own caste, you hope that Krishnan will do so.

If Krishnan leaves, there will be fewer people trying to share the limited sandalmaking business. There will be a better chance for you to support a family of your own. And if Krishnan finds out that a good life is possible in a strange place and outside the caste, you may seriously consider following him and doing the same.

You are going to try to convince your brother to go and to convince your father that it would be a good idea.

Ravi Bedavar

You are a leader of the brotherhood of sandalmakers. This is an informal community of people of the same caste who help each other at ceremonial times, like weddings and burials. Your group also sees to it that people respect and obey the rules of the caste.

You have heard that Krishnan Rojatli is thinking of moving away and trying a different trade outside the caste. You must warn him what a mistake that would be.

You can remind him how important a properly arranged marriage and properly conducted burials are to a Hindu family. These things can only be done by the brotherhood of caste members. How would it look if there were a funeral and no caste members to handle it and do the proper things?

If a traditional family like the Rojatlis were to leave the caste, it would show serious weakness in the system. You must try to talk Krishnan out of the idea.

LIRA NAKTAL

You are a nurse at the health clinic that serves a number of villages, including the one in which the Rojatlis live. Although you come from the city of Bombay, you know that at one time your family were members of the same caste as the Rojatlis. But the rules and customs of caste are not so important in Bombay. There, you were able to get an education and a government job.

You feel that caste traditions have held back the full development of India's people. You are particularly impressed by some of Krishnan and Santha's children, whom you have treated at the clinic. They are bright and talented. You would like to see them get full educations and consider careers beyond sandal-making.

As a woman, you cannot make a direct suggestion to Krishnan in a traditional village. Still, you will try to influence Santha to work for the move to the city.

SANGEETA ROJATLI

You are the oldest daughter of Krishnan and Santha Rojatli. You were sick for a long time a year ago and had to make many visits to the health clinic. You were very impressed by Nurse Naktal at the clinic, who seemed to know a lot about health and medicine. You decided that you also might like to become a nurse, but your parents told you that such a career is not possible in your caste. You will be married to a man who works with leather and animal skins—perhaps a sandalmaker like your father. You cannot volunteer to help at the clinic, because higher caste people will not let you handle things they use.

You want your parents to go someplace where there are no caste restrictions. You will try to show them that it would make life so much better for their children.

BIBLIOGRAPHY

Chellaney, Brahma. "Passage to Power." *World Monitor*, February 1990.

Cohen, Bernard S. *India: Social Anthropology of a Civilization*. New York: Prentice-Hall, 1975.

Dumont, Louis. *Homo Hierarchieus: The Caste System and Its Implications*. Chicago: University of Chicago Press, 1970.

Holmes, Fred. *India: Focus on Change*. New York: Prentice-Hall, 1975.

Isaacs, Harold. *India's Ex-Untouchables*. New York: Harper & Row, 1974.

Johnson, Donald J., and Jean E. Johnson, eds. *Through Indian Eyes: The Wheel of Life*. New York: Praeger, 1991.

Mehta, Ved. "Letter from New Delhi." *The New Yorker*, March 1991.

Norton, James H.K. *The Third World: South Asia*. Guilford, CT: Dushkin, 1984.

Srinivas, M.N. *Social Change in Modern India*. Berkeley: The University of California Press, 1981.

Tudisco, A. Jeff. *Class and Caste in Village India*. San Francisco: Field, 1969.

Zinkin, Taya. *Caste Today*. London: Oxford University Press, 1962.

SOUTHEAST ASIA

Extended or Nuclear Family Living?

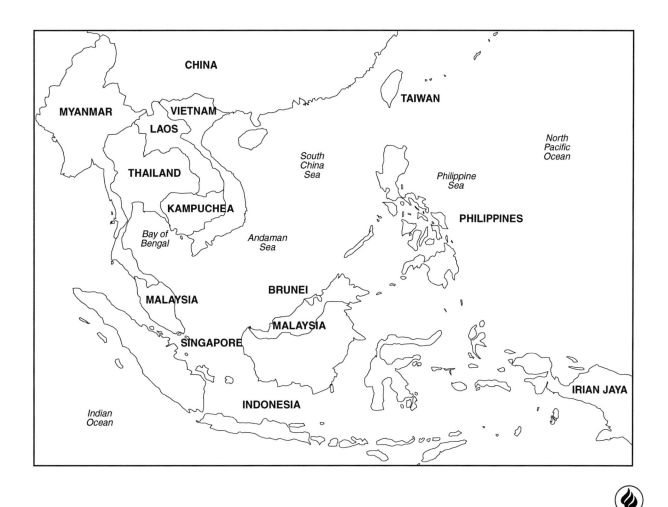

BACKGROUND

The extended family is the dominant pattern throughout the Third World. However, pressures created by industrialization, urbanization, and exposure to other lifestyles have challenged the commitment to building life around extended families.

In Southeast Asia, the extended family has long been the standard. This is particularly true of Indonesia, where housing construction design has been committed to the extended family pattern. Modern urban housing as well as traditional village houses are designed with extra bedrooms to accommodate these customs.

The case study presents the impulse for pulling back to the nuclear family as more advanced than it generally is. Indonesians are still overwhelmingly devoted to living as extended families. Nevertheless, the case study provides an appropriate situation for this society as well as a great many other communities around the world.

SCENARIO

Achmed Kanoto is a clerk in the Jakarta office of an Indonesian shipping company. He and his wife, Rusiah, have been living in part of his cousin's house while they save money for their own home. Achmed has a steady job, but it does not pay very well. He does not have enough training to be promoted to an executive job in the company.

The Kanotos have learned there is a house for sale not far away. They could buy it with their savings, but it is small. It has only enough room for themselves and their children.

In Indonesia most people live in *extended* families. A husband, wife, and children will have relatives like uncles, aunts, and brothers living with them. Many people build houses with extra bedrooms so kinfolk can live there too, and with large verandahs to entertain many guests.

For the Kanotos, the decision whether to wait until they can afford a larger house is complicated. It is a choice about whether to continue the extended family tradition or to change to living mainly as a nuclear family, as "Westerners" do.

(NOTE: Some of the characters in this simulation have only a single name. In Indonesia, some people have first and last names and some only one name.)

ACHMED KANOTO

You are a clerk in a large office in Jakarta, the capital city of Indonesia. You have a high school education, but your job with a shipping company has enabled you to travel to other parts of Southeast Asia. You and your wife, Rusiah, have two children.

You have been living with your cousin Ali and contributing some money every month for Ali's household expenses. But you have also made other sacrifices so that you could one day have your own home. Now you see the announcement of small, inexpensive houses for sale not far away.

A home of your own is important to you. But you have always lived in large houses, big enough to accommodate relatives as well as your own nuclear family. Buying the small house would mean turning away from the extended family tradition.

RUSIAH KANOTO

You are married to Achmed Kanoto. The two of you and your children live in his cousin's house in Jakarta, Indonesia. Although your husband grew up in an extended family, your own parents had a shop in a town where they had no relatives. There, you got used to nuclear family life.

Now a small house is for sale nearby, and Achmed is considering buying it. You know that he hesitates only because the house does not have room for visiting relatives. But you would like to have again the privacy you knew when you lived with your parents. Then, you did not have a lot of people involved in everything you did.

You will try to convince Achmed to buy the smaller house.

MUHAMMED KANOTO

You are Achmed Kanoto's father. You still live in the Kanoto family's ancestral village, in a large house with many relatives. You do not see Achmed so often since he went to work in Jakarta. Still, he writes regular letters and brings his family back to the village for holiday visits.

You are especially proud of the extra large verandah that your sons built onto your house. Now you can entertain large groups of relatives and friends. Family contacts are very important to you. You are pleased that Achmed and his family have been living among your relatives in the city.

In his last letter, Achmed reported that he has a chance to buy his own house. But the home would be too small for any relatives to live with him or make long visits. He said that he would like to talk the idea over with you on his next visit.

You think it would be a serious mistake for Achmed to move to the small house. You will tell him so as soon as you can.

ALI KANOTO

You are Achmed's cousin. You are pleased and proud that he and his family have lived with you ever since they arrived in Jakarta. Extended families living together have always been attractive to you. You cannot understand why Achmed would even consider moving to a smaller house.

You realize that a big city like Jakarta is a place of rapid change. New apartment houses and office buildings are being added every week. But you think this rapid change is all the more reason to hold on to old traditions, like living together with relatives.

You will tell your cousin Achmed not to live apart from his kinfolk.

PIDENOGO

You are a clerk in the same office as Achmed Kanoto. Like Achmed, you live with relatives, and you expect to continue doing so permanently. It is nice to be among many people who care about you and are part of the same family.

The money you give your relatives toward house expenses is much less than it would cost to buy or rent your own home. You can spend the difference on clothing and entertainment. Your life would be much more limited if you had to put a lot of your income into housing.

You will try to talk Achmed into staying on where he is, with his relatives.

KALAMBITAN

You are a friend of Achmed Kanoto. You have an apartment in one of the new buildings in Jakarta. But it is an extra large apartment, with rooms for some cousins who live with you. You know that Achmed is now looking for a home of his own.

You enjoy having your cousins with you. Now that you are in the big city, you miss having all your relatives nearby. In your village there were many aunts, uncles, cousins, and others who knew you well. They were always interested in what you and your family were doing. But in Jakarta, the other people in the apartment building are strangers, although they are friendly. It makes a big difference to have relatives living with you.

You will suggest that Achmed either wait until he can afford a larger house or move into a large apartment. You think it would be a great mistake for him not to stay close to his extended family.

Maria Samrin

You are a public health nurse in Jakarta. The Kanoto family comes to your clinic from time to time. Rusiah Kanoto has told you of her interest in a home of her own, away from the constant company of her husband's relatives.

You disagree with Mrs. Kanoto's attitude. You think that the commitment to extended families is one of those important things that gives Indonesia its special character. You were recently part of a medical delegation from Indonesia that attended a conference in the Netherlands. There, you were appalled to find that people were separated from most of their relatives. They had little idea of what was happening daily among any relatives beyond the nuclear family.

You want to talk to the Kanotos. You plan to tell them how important it is to live in a way that keeps the extended family together.

Sutan Hattma

You are an official in the shipping company that employs Achmed Kanoto. You have admired Achmed's good work habits. You have been friendly, sometimes offering advice on personal matters. You have now heard that Achmed is thinking of buying a small house for his own (nuclear) family and moving away from his relatives.

You think it would be an excellent idea for Achmed to do so. At one time, you had some of your own extended family living with you. You did not like it. It seemed to you that the young men among your cousins were lazy. As long as they had your nice house to live in, they saw no reason to look hard for work and to try to better their lives. At the same time, they were always around. You had to include them in any plans you and your wife wanted to make.

You will advise Achmed to move out on his own and separate from the extended family.

FATIMAH HATTMA

You are the wife of Sutan Hattma, who is one of the officials of the shipping company at which Achmed Kanoto works. You and your husband used to have a number of Sutan's relatives living with you, but you grew tired of it.

It seemed that the relatives were always around, although they were quite pleasant. You could never feel right about doing things without including them. Since your husband is a rising success at the company, you have had to entertain some of the company wives on occasion. When you did, you were embarrassed by the relatives. They were around the house and would not fit in with the company people.

You will advise Rusiah Kanoto to urge her husband to get away from the extended family situation and into their own house.

AGUS DOMO

You are a house builder in the city of Jakarta. You do not have enough capital to put up large houses or apartment buildings. So you have to come up with the idea of building a few small houses at a time. You can use the profits to expand your business.

You know that Achmed Kanoto is popular with his fellow workers. Many people will pay attention to what he does. So you will make a special effort to get the Kanotos to buy the small house. You can emphasize the low price and the fact that a small house is easy to keep up. The idea is not yet the standard. The Kanotos can get one of the small houses cheaply, before they become very popular and the price goes up.

BIBLIOGRAPHY

Chamratrithining, Apichat, et al., "Living Arrangements and Family Formation in Thailand." *Social Forces*, June 1988.

Fersh, Seymour. *Asia: Teaching About/Learning From.* New York: Teachers College Press, 1978.

McVey, Ruth, ed. *Indonesia.* New York: Taplinger, 1963.

Neill, Wilfred. *Twentieth Century Indonesia.* New York: Columbia University Press, 1973.

Osborne, Milton. *Southeast Asia: An Introductory History.* London: Allen and Unwin, 1979.

Rockowitz, Murray, ed. *Family.* New York: Scholastic, 1969.

Smith, Datus C. *The Land and People of Indonesia.* New York: Lippincott, 1983.

Swearer, Donald K. *The Third World: Southeast Asia.* Guilford, CT. Dushkin, 1984.

Thompson, Carol, ed. *Southeast Asia.* Philadelphia: Current History, 1984.

Williams, Lea E. *Southeast Asia: A History.* New York: Oxford University Press, 1976.

RUSSIA AND THE COMMONWEALTH OF INDEPENDENT STATES

Guiding Principles in a Time of Transition

BACKGROUND

The 1991 collapse of Communist Party authority over the Soviet Union led to an extraordinary explosion of ideological forces. The Russian people confronted many ideas long suppressed by the Soviet regime—religion, capitalism, monarchism, democracy, and ethnic diversity, among others. Within the Commonwealth of Independent States, different ideological impulses may now hold different priorities: in the Central Asian republics, for example, Islam is re-emerging as a significant factor. For this case study, however, we shall focus on the most important part of the former Soviet Union, the Russian Republic.

There the continuing economic crisis and its accompanying general breakdown in such areas as crime control, resource allocation, and the availability of consumer goods has undermined confidence in the emerging democratic system. At the same time, emotional dislocation is fed by the frustration of losing the superpower status that had earned the USSR respect, if not admiration, from other nations.

It can therefore be useful to use this opportunity to explore how and why people in crisis may be drawn to authoritarian and totalitarian as well as democratic solutions. The Bolshevik dictatorship, after all, replaced not an authoritarian society but the 1917 provisional government that was as democratic as any European government of its time.

Although the issue of loss of superpower status is of special importance to the Russians, other issues of the disarray following the collapse of totalitarianism would apply to any formerly Communist country. The issue of antidemocratic impulses in a poorly performing economy could also apply to any culture.

SCENARIO

Boris Perchov is a former Red Army colonel, who was forced into early retirement when the withdrawal of Soviet troops from Eastern Europe created a surplus of military forces. He and his family are now crowded into a small, poorly furnished Moscow apartment, where he finds that his military pension does not keep up with the rising cost of living.

Boris feels that his personal problems reflect those of Russia itself. In addition to economic concerns, his status has changed dramatically. While he is now another pensioner standing in line for scarce products, he used to be a symbol of power and privilege. The East German people treated him with respect, and perhaps fear, when his regiment was stationed there. As a colonel, he had access to the best of housing, consumer products, and such benefits as restricted recreational facilities.

The simulated discussion takes place at a picnic of fellow military retirees and their families. All of them are dismayed by their current situation. They and their relatives are considering what solution might be best for them and for Russia.

BORIS PERCHOV

You are fifty years old and recently retired from your post as commander of a tank regiment in what had been the army of the Soviet Union. You have returned to Moscow, where you and your wife have relatives. Your two children are college students—Ivan has been doing graduate studies in space engineering, and Vera has been preparing to be an elementary school art teacher. Your pension barely covers food and rent, so you are looking for some employment, but have training only in the military. Your wife has not worked for many years, but is now trying to get a job that makes use of her cooking skills.

As a colonel, you had many privileges. The army provided you with good housing, including servants, and you enjoyed the special facilities—stores, medical and recreational facilities, and so on—set aside for high-ranking officers. You also liked the special respect given a Red Army colonel by the public in your country and by local people in the different parts of Eastern Europe where your regiment was stationed.

You feel especially bitter about the fact that you gave thirty years of total loyalty to the government, never challenging an order—such as your difficult service in Afghanistan in the 1980's—with the expectation that in return the government would provide you with a comfortable retirement. Instead, your retirement is plagued by insecurity and the possibility of hunger.

At the same time, you know that the soldiers you commanded in Afghanistan returned, in the old Soviet Union, to lives without privileges or personal freedom. For them, the Communist system had failed. What now should replace it?

IVAN PERCHOV

You are almost finished with your program of advanced studies in space engineering. This is a very specialized and demanding program, but until recently people who completed this training were guaranteed positions in the USSR's space program. Now many space facilities have been shut down and many workers have been dismissed, because the program was mostly focused on military activities that are no longer supported. The civilian part of the program is considered too expensive. Your professors tell you it is extremely unlikely that you will be able to find any work in the field for which you have been training.

You had been looking forward to this career since you were a small child. Many Russian children were so excited by Soviet space achievements that they dreamed of becoming space scientists, but the training was so difficult that very few could even try. Indeed, keeping up with your studies meant sacrificing most of the usual activities of students and young adults. But you thought it would be worth it to be part of one of the world's greatest programs.

Your friends offer a range of advice. Some suggest that Russia should go back to what it was a few years ago—a great power that was capable of maintaining a space program rivaling that of the United States—even better than the American program in some areas. Others say that it was unrealistic to commit so many resources to space when the economy had failed to provide the basic needs that a citizen of Western Europe or the United States could take for granted.

Are you prepared to make great personal sacrifices to perhaps build a Russia with a better life for all, or are you interested in a return to old priorities that would value all your years of training?

VERA PERCHOV

You are a student at an art institute, and your own interest is in becoming an art teacher. As a result, your friends include people who are interested in Russian and world art as well as people who are studying education and are very interested in world affairs. Some of your friends were personally involved in the demonstrations in 1991 that led to the overthrow of the Communist government. Most were not actually there, but are delighted by the disappearance of a system that stood for censorship and resistance to fundamental change.

You know that most of your family were committed to working within the old system; your father and brother had dedicated their careers to it. You can see how hard it is for your parents to adjust to the great loss of the privileges that your father's outstanding military service had earned for them; that is especially hard to accept.

But you and your friends are excited by the prospect of real freedom. In your own field, it means exploring the kinds of art that appeal to you without having to find out if some government or Communist Party official will even allow you to think about it. Your Russian pride was stimulated when you learned there were great Russian artists who did their work in the West because it was banned in the Soviet Union.

You want to convince your parents that despite their personal losses, the changes in Russia offer a great future.

OLGA PERCHOV

You have spent most of your adult life as the wife of Boris Perchov, an officer in the army of the Soviet Union. Now the withdrawal of that army from Eastern Europe and its great reduction in size have resulted in the forced retirement of your husband, who is only fifty years old.

Your own life has changed enormously. A few years ago, you had a lovely home on the military base, with servants and with special privileges, such as access to special stores, that shielded you from the difficulties of everyday life endured by most of the Soviet people.

Now you live in a small, crowded apartment. The rapid increases in the cost of living have made your husband's military pension barely enough to provide daily food. You have thought about your own skills, and hope that your ability as a cook will perhaps lead to a job in a restaurant or hotel.

Your daughter, Vera, is an art student and seems really excited about the new freedom in Russia. She sympathizes with your problems but is thrilled by the prospect of living in freedom. On the other hand, your son, Ivan, has been studying for years to become a space scientist. Russia's new priorities for consumer goods mean that he probably cannot have the career he always expected and worked so hard for.

You unquestioningly followed your husband wherever the army sent him. Now those years of duty have led to a shabby apartment in a poor section of Moscow, and the comfortable retirement you always expected cannot be counted upon.

Should you share your daughter's excitement about the new Russia, or listen to those who say that things have gone too far in destroying the old Soviet Union?

LEONID MIRKICH

You were Boris Perchov's classmate in the military academy, and you have remained friends even when your military careers kept you apart. Like Boris, you were forced to retire early when the Soviet Union was cut back to the Russian Republic and its army greatly reduced.

The army was the most important thing in your life, and you have had a hard time adjusting to civilian life. It is especially hard for you to adjust to the changed attitude of the rest of the people and of other nations towards the army. Last week, you wore your uniform for a veterans' ceremony, and some teenage German tourists asked if you would sell them your medals as souvenirs. You remember when you wore your uniform in East Germany and people there were extra respectful to you.

You have heard about new political groups that are forming in Russia. Some have pledged to undo the government's military cutbacks and restore the power and prestige that made the Red Army respected around the world. You want to suggest to Boris that you and he contact that group; you must show him why he should.

VLADIMIR PERCHOV

You are the brother of Boris Perchov. You have spent your career in the Moscow Police Department and are now a senior official there. Now that your brother has returned from the army, you want to tell him what has been going on and talk about what to do.

Since the breakdown of the authority of the old system, there has been an enormous increase in all kinds of crime. This is especially true of what Americans call "organized crime," or people in Italy call the Mafia—powerful criminal organizations that commit armed robberies on businesses and threaten other businesses with the same fate unless they make "protection" payments to the gangsters.

When the Communist Party and the KGB (State Security Police) held absolute power, criminals would never have dared be so brazen. Now the combination of new limits on police power and a general loss of respect for authority have made criminals bolder than ever. You really wonder if they can be controlled under the new democracy.

You want Boris to join those who say the changes have gone too far and who call for a return to a strong central authority that would restore law and order.

ALEXANDER DARETSKY

You are a general in the Russian army and were Boris Perchov's commanding officer before he was forced to retire. You consider him an outstanding officer and are upset that men of such proven ability had to leave when the size of the armed forces was so heavily cut.

You are unhappy with the new Russian army. It is much smaller than the old army of the Soviet Union, and, of course, is responsible for a much smaller country. You enjoyed the power and prestige of the old Red Army and took great pride in the way it was able to assert Russian power along its borders and throughout Eastern Europe. Now all of those separate nationalities—Ukraine, Belarus, Kazhakstan, etc.—have broken away and set up their own armed forces. The disciplined power that forced the world to accommodate Russia's interests has shattered.

It took centuries for Russia, under the Czars and under the Communist Party, to bring under its control all the strategic areas on its borders. Now Russia's borders are again vulnerable; it is clear that the new leaders lack the will to send out troops to regain the lost regions. Some kind of strong national leadership, using military discipline, could provide that will, and you have been talking to current and recent officers about a military takeover.

Colonel Perchov's reputation as a hero and respected leader of troops would be a big help to your group. You want to convince Boris that Russia's best hope is a military takeover. You will appeal to his sense of what Russia used to be and show him that strong leadership by the military is the way to return to greatness.

Maya Dorovna

You are Colonel Perchov's mother-in-law. You are eighty-three years old and have witnessed life under the Czar, the revolutions, the civil war, Stalin's brutality, the Nazi invasion, and the changes in communism that finally produced the breakup of the USSR. You believe that what enabled you to survive all this was your commitment to the Russian Orthodox religion. You kept it secret for many years, at first because of official persecution, and later because your daughter's husband was an army officer and it might have caused him problems.

Now you are delighted to practice your religion openly, and you are thrilled by the crowds that are now coming to churches that used to be nearly empty, or closed altogether. Your daughter has gone with you a few times lately, and you would like to get the colonel to also attend.

You know that your children and their friends have been talking about the political, economic, and moral crises that have beset Russia since the overthrow of the Communist system. They are seeking some set of beliefs that could bring the country back to responsible and constructive behavior.

It is obvious to you that the answer is a revival of the old Orthodox church. You are aware that there could be some problems with that. The priests are a mixture of people who would like to bring back the royal family (the Czar had been the official head of the church), people who got their positions when the Communists were in power and were accepted because they never criticized the dictatorial, atheistic Party, and people who really see Orthodoxy as a spiritual base for the moral guidance of the Russian people. The last group—the spiritual leaders—represent for you the best hope for Russia.

You want to convince the colonel and your daughter to join the church and to use it to spread the old values that had made Russia great.

ANATOL GOORVICH

You are an old friend of Colonel Perchov. You were in the same army unit in the war in Afghanistan in the 1980's, until you were badly wounded there and had to return to civilian life. During your years of recuperation, you became very bitter, particularly about the fact that the public never showed you and other wounded veterans the kind of appreciation you deserved. After all of the sacrifices made by you and your comrades, the politicians withdrew from Afghanistan under Western pressure, abandoning the Communist government you had fought so heroically to protect.

It seems clear to you that Russia's politicians have sold out to Western interests. They have no commitment to the natural role of Russia as a great power dominating the peoples of Eastern Europe and Central Asia. It looks as if the only ones to have benefited by the breakup of the USSR are Western capitalists, who now have access to the resources of those areas, and the Jews, who have been able to remove the Soviet Union as a protector of Arab nations in the Middle East.

You have read pamphlets and heard speeches about the historic alliance of international capitalism and Judaism to take over the world. It has been Russia's historic role, under the Czars and then under the Communist Party, to destroy that conspiracy. That role made Russia great, and put other peoples— Ukrainians, Lithuanians, Armenians, and so on—in their proper place under the control of the great Russian people.

You want to convince the Perchov family to join your movement to clean out the international capitalists, Jews, and self-interested politicians, and get behind a strong leader who will restore the true greatness of Mother Russia.

NATASHA SPENSKA

You are Vera Perchov's best friend. You are in your final year at the university and are looking forward to being a school teacher. You took part in the demonstrations in 1991 that led to the overthrow of the Communist system, and feel that that was the most important thing you ever did. You remember how excited all of the students had been by the spirit of *glasnost*, the opening up of the Soviet Union to new ideas and a more honest look at the past. You knew then that Russia had a great future, once it got rid of the rigid Communist dictatorship.

Of course, the needed changes have not been easy on the people. There have been terrible shortages of things people need most, and there seem to be great inequalities. Some are able to get very rich under the new freedom and others have sunk to miserable poverty. There is also continuing violence between different ethnic groups as they struggle to dominate parts of what had been one unified nation.

But no country has ever been able to move from dictatorship to democracy without some sacrifices. Even the inequalities that now exist are based on some people's ability to take advantage of opportunities more quickly, instead of the old system in which the best of everything was reserved for the Communist leadership while everyone else suffered. You also do not believe that Russia had any right to rule other peoples, either as occupied nations like East Germany or as forced parts of the USSR like Latvia.

You are sorry that Vera's father lost so much when the army cut a lot of officers, but you expect to help Vera convince her parents that Russia will have a better future once the temporary problems are overcome.

BIBLIOGRAPHY

Botkin, L. "Which Route for Russia?" *World Press Review,* February 1992.

Cole, Robert A., and Janet G. Vaillant, eds. *Activities for Teaching Russian and Soviet Studies in the High School.* Boulder, CO: Social Science Education Consortium, 1990.

Edwards, M. "Russia Today." *National Geographic,* March 1993.

Elliott, D. "We Need Law and Order: Russia's Armed Forces and the Political Crisis." *Newsweek,* April 5, 1993.

Erlanger, Steven. "In Choppy Russian Economy, a Family Jury-Rigs a Budget." *The New York Times,* July 20, 1992.

Finan, William Jr., ed. "The Second Russian Revolution." *Current History,* October 1992.

Hingley, Ronald. *The Russian Mind.* New York: Scribner's, 1977.

Shipler, David K. *Russia: Broken Idols, Solemn Dreams.* New York: Times Books, 1983.

Solomon, Andrew. "Young Russia's Defiant Decadence." *The New York Times Magazine,* July 18, 1993.

Steel, Suzanne. "Tractors Plow Field of Capitalist Dreams." *The Columbus Dispatch,* July 17, 1992.

White, Stephen. "Russia's Experiment with Democracy." *Current History,* October 1992.

WESTERN EUROPE

The Role of Foreign Workers

BACKGROUND

Although this simulation is set in Germany, the situation is important for a large part of Western Europe; similar discussions are being held in Switzerland, France, and The Netherlands, among other nations. The sources of foreign workers vary among most countries, but the majority of the workers have come from Italy, Spain, Greece, Turkey, Yugoslavia, and North Africa. In Germany, nearly one half of the work force is made up of foreign workers. Most of them return to their homes at the conclusion of job contracts, but a majority of the Turks and Yugoslavs have remained. When a recession and the great costs of integrating East Germany into a united Germany combined to increase German unemployment, physical attacks on foreign workers, especially Turks, increased and were encouraged by extreme right-wing groups. Various responses—from repatriation to integration—have been considered by the host government. It is a profound social and economic issue for Germany and, to varying degrees, for other European nations.

The obvious parallel for Americans is the role of Mexican workers in the United States. Various programs, including ignoring the issue, trying to regulate the flow (as in the now-defunct "bracero" program), and trying to close the borders to all but official immigrants have been tried. In the 1990's the question of migrant workers became a major topic in congressional debate over immigration reform. Students may be interested in directly examining the American situation or considering what aspects of the German experience might be applicable to the United States.

SCENARIO

Helga Tobler is a writer for a popular magazine in Germany. Her new assignment is to gather opinions on the future of foreign workers in her country. She has decided to interview a wide range of people on the topic.

She has had some contact with foreign workers over the years. Her parents' restaurant has employed many foreigners, ranging from the chef, who is a refugee from Hungary, to the busboys, who are usually from Turkey. Through these people Helga has met foreign workers and become friendly enough to hold serious conversations about their lives.

She has also talked to her own friends and relatives to find out what their impressions are. As a professional writer, she is usually able to draw out other people's ideas without having to give her own opinion.

Her editor suggests that a personal point of view would probably stir more interest among readers. Helga, however, feels that she should not make up her mind in advance.

HELGA TOBLER

You have had a successful career as a feature writer for magazines. Now you have your own column and will use it to discuss important issues.

Although you grew up in West Germany and still live there, you have traveled to many parts of the world. Your work as a journalist has taught you a lot about how the world looks to different kinds of people.

The article about foreign workers will be especially important. It will be your first column about a serious subject. Your editor will be watching closely to see how readers like it. You want to show that you can organize the key arguments and produce a reasonable solution.

But you have to decide: Should your own suggestion be the best idea, even if most of your German readers might disagree?

HEINRICH GATZKE

You are a union organizer for West German transport workers. You feel that wages of your union members are held down by the many people from poorer countries who are willing to work for low wages. You are sure that cutting down sharply on immigration would raise German wages.

You have to explain to Helga Tobler how you and the members of your union feel.

GERTRUDE TOBLER

You are Helga's mother and have put a lot of work into the family restaurant that is now quite successful. You know that one thing your customers appreciate is the high standard of service you provide. No one's water glass remains empty for more than a few seconds before someone appears at the table with a cool refill.

Your waiters and busboys are from Turkey and Yugoslavia. Although it has been hard to teach them basic German, you have found them to be hardworking and responsible. Hiring local German workers would be quite expensive. It might even force you to raise prices to the point where you would lose customers.

GUNTHER MEINZ

You work for the German government in the Department of Migrant Workers. You support the use of foreign workers, but you are worried about the problems of controlling immigration. Migrant workers need services such as medical and educational programs. You feel that the publicity given to illegal immigration may encourage people to think these services are too expensive because of use by illegal immigrants.

You want laws against illegal immigration strictly enforced, including deporting of illegal immigrants. But you believe in protecting all the rights of legal immigrants.

KARL PROTT

You are a member of the local city council and are looking forward to holding national office in Germany. You are finding that speeches for more limits on immigration get a lot of applause from many voters. You want to see Germany's wealth used to improve the life of Germans, not to give privileges to foreigners.

Some foreign workers may be necessary for the labor supply, but their numbers should be restricted as much as possible. You call for issuing passports only to workers without families and limiting the number of years such workers can stay. You also want to increase greatly the penalties for illegal immigration and for helping people enter illegally.

PETER HELLMAN

You are a German police official. It seems to you that every month you capture and deport hundreds of illegal aliens. Still, more are arriving than you can control. As long as so many illegal residents are in the immigrant communities, it is hard to locate criminals and control unlawful activities. It is also easy for people to involve others in crime. Illegal residents are afraid to have anything to do with the police.

It also bothers you that young hoodlums who attack Turks are sometimes cheered by respectable citizens who would otherwise never tolerate them.

You believe it might be worthwhile to declare an amnesty—to provide legal recognition to all who have lived here for a long time. This could make legality and cooperation the accepted way in immigrant neighborhoods and would help police work.

Senta Rogar

As the mother of young children, you pay a lot of attention to the schools. Now you are worried about changes in your local school. About a quarter of the students in the school district are immigrants. It seems to you that they have brought too many alterations to the schools. These children do not speak German and require special classes. Their habits and styles seem very strange, including their Moslem religion. The teachers have to give a lot of extra attention to the foreign students, and this means less is available for your own children. Somehow, the pattern has to be changed.

Dietrich Meyer

You are the spokesman for the restaurant owners' association. Your members have supported the idea of bringing in large numbers of foreign workers. You have discussed the subject with the leaders of other business associations. You agree that Germany's economy has now become dependent on these workers. There are nearly five million foreign workers. If they were to be sent home, the country's economic system would fail.

MUSTAFA GABRIZ

You have been a trash collector for the city for five years. You are making much more money than you could have made in Ankara, your home city in Turkey. Last year, you felt that your job was secure enough to bring your family here. Now you all live together in Germany.

Some of your friends talk about staying here, but you plan to work only long enough to have the savings to buy a house in Turkey. Then you will return home. Your job is not bad, but you miss your old lifestyle—Turkish stores, cafés, and places to relax with fellow Turks. You particularly miss your parents and other relatives.

You hope that the laws regulating foreign workers will be made more liberal so other workers and their families can come to Germany.

SORAYA GABRIZ

You are the wife of Mustafa Gabriz, who works as a trash collector. Your husband left Ankara, your home in Turkey, six years ago to find work in West Germany. He has had a steady job for the last five years. Last year he brought you and your children to Germany to join him.

Your life in Germany is much better than the poverty you had in Turkey. But you can see many problems for the foreign workers, many of whom cannot bring their families in to join them. You and Mustafa plan to return to Turkey as soon as you have saved enough money. But you are still concerned about life for Turks and other foreign workers in Germany.

You feel that the foreign workers do a lot of the most difficult, unpleasant, and low-paying jobs. In return, Germany should make it easier for foreign workers to come and go and to bring their families to live with them.

BIBLIOGRAPHY

Abercrombie, Thomas. "Unsettled Immigrants." *National Geographic*, July 1989.

Grapin, Jacqueline. "Our Borders Are Like a Sieve." *World Paper*, February 1984.

Hoffman, George W. *A Geography of Europe: Problems and Prospects*. New York: Wiley, 1977.

Jackson, James. "Ethnic Conflict in the Global Village: Probing the Nature of Xenophobia and Racism." *University of Michigan Research News*, Winter 1992.

Kennedy, Brenner. *Foreign Workers and Immigration Policy: The Case of France*. Washington: OECD, 1980.

Kinzer, Stephen. "Germany's Young Turks Say 'Enough' to the Bias." *The New York Times*, June 6, 1993.

Power, Jonathan. *Migrant Workers in Western Europe and the United States*. New York: Pergamon, 1979.

Ramai, Sonia. "Children in Nomansland: The Dilemma of Second Generation Immigrants." *UNESCO Courier*, 1984.

Taylor, Paul. *The Limits of European Integration*. New York: Columbia University Press, 1983.

NORTH AFRICA AND THE MIDDLE EAST

Women's Roles in a Traditional Society

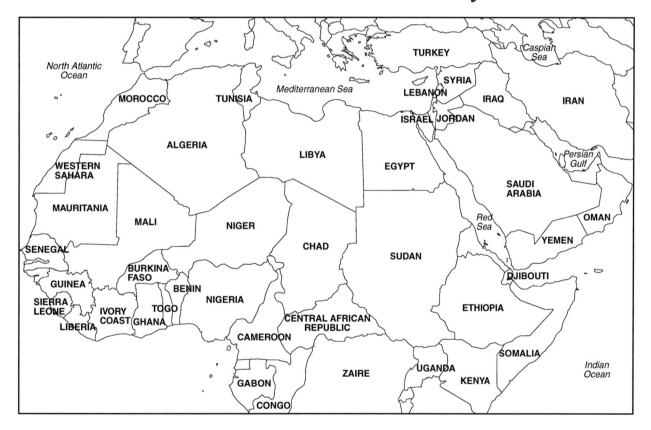

BACKGROUND

This case study focuses on the question of higher education for women in a traditional Middle Eastern culture—in this case, the Druze people of the Galilee.

The Druze are Arabs, most of them living in three countries—Syria, Lebanon, and Israel. Their culture is based on their unique religion, which separated from Islam in the eleventh century. They have fought bitter battles over the centuries with Christians and Moslems to defend their cultural autonomy.

Druze values are perhaps best summed up in a statement made to Rafik Halaby, an Israeli Druze journalist, by his father: "Do not sell your land, and protect your sister's honor." Attachment to the land is profound; families generally stay in the same village for generations (and are deeply involved with their neighbors). The concept of female honor is also very important. Honor is a family idea among the Druze, as among most traditional Arab peoples.

The *hamula*, or extended family, is keenly aware of the activities of all its members, who take pride in the accomplishments of all and can be hurt by the failure of any. If a member does something that besmirches the family honor, all of the relatives may suffer; all are, accordingly, concerned when anything threatens their honor.

Among the traditional people, there is no way a young woman can live among outsiders and be considered a woman of honor. A young girl is expected to have her future bridegroom selected by arrangements between the parents (she can only marry a Druze). Until her marriage, the protection of her honor is the sacred duty of her brothers and her father.

Some Druze women in Lebanon, and a few in Israel, have found acceptance as individuals involved in public activities outside their parents' villages, but this is very rare among the traditional people in the Galilee mountains. It is a difficult issue, because modernization is now appearing in that district.

Since 1960, electricity has come to the region and, together with a steadily growing economy, has resulted in the availability of home appliances and services that can liberate women from their traditional limits as cooks and mothers. But the freedom thus won can undermine the network of traditions that has enabled the Druze people to maintain a distinctive unified culture in a region dominated by potential enemies.

SCENARIO

Fawzia Haroun is a seventeen-year-old Druze girl living in the village of Fetya in Upper Galilee, Israel. Her father, Ali Haroun, is the principal of the Fetya elementary school. He has a high school education and has attended a teacher training institution in Haifa. Fawzia's mother, Nuria, has an elementary school education and has been a housewife all her married life. Fawzia is one of seven girls who will graduate this year from the regional Druze high school in Bet Ja'an.

The faculty of the Bet Ja'an High School had informed the family that Fawzia received the highest marks of any student at the school. The teachers know that no girl from the Druze mountain villages has ever gone to college. Now they suggest it might be time to change the tradition. They will be willing to handle the arrangements if Fawzia's family supports the idea of her enrolling.

Maryam, a Christian Arab girl from Fetya, has decided to go to Haifa University. She has asked Fawzia to go also, so there will be someone else at college from the same village. The Haroun family is considering the idea.

ALI HAROUN

You have a high school education and were the first member of your generation in Fetya to receive one. Your position as a school principal is very prestigious. You are also very aware that your family is one of the most prominent in the village. Everything you do is therefore the subject of some interest to everyone in the community.

You are proud of your daughter Fawzia's academic achievement. But you do not feel easy about a Druze woman leaving her village and going to a coeducational school among non-Druze people. No woman from this region has ever done that. Many traditionalists will consider such an action as dishonoring the family. As the eldest son, it is your responsibility to protect the honor of your family. Personally, Fawzia's going to college does not necessarily seem dishonorable to you.

You have seen nearby Arab women who have obtained secular education and have then rejected the traditional values of their people. You think that Fawzia has strong loyalty to traditional Druze values. However, you are not sure if that could change.

NURIA HAROUN

You are especially proud of your daughter Fawzia's academic success. You were the brightest student in your own elementary school. Your parents, though, would not spend the money to further educate a girl when boys had to be schooled. Therefore, you have a special interest in supporting your daughter's desire to continue her education.

Nevertheless, you must be sensitive to the fact that criticism will be aimed at your husband's family. You came from a family of another village. This makes it awkward to urge an action that could create problems for the Haroun family.

Fawzia Haroun

It took a lot of hard work to earn outstanding grades in Bet Ja'an while carrying a full share of family chores at home. You are excited by the reports of your cousin, a Lebanese Druze girl who has gone to college. You want to do the same. You know there is a great shortage of college-educated Druze. You want to be able to help educate your own people.

Your family is extremely important in your life, and you expect to marry someone from Bet Ja'an. You hope that your family will understand that your desire for a college education is not intended as an attack upon their way of life.

Yusuf Haroun

You are Fawzia's grandfather and are one of the most prominent men in the village. Thirty years ago, you were mayor of Fetya.

You are eighty years old. From 1925 to 1945, you were a soldier in the British army. You served in the Transjordan Frontier Force and the Arab Legion (the main unit of the Jordanian army, at that time commanded by British officers). You received a medical discharge because of war wounds. You then retired to your family's home village of Fetya in Upper Galilee.

You know a good deal about Western ways from your military service, as well as from living in Israel. But you feel strongly for tradition. You are delighted that your grandson Daoud is studying for a religious life. You are also quite proud of the fact that your family is well educated.

You have always felt that woman's place is in the home.

SAMIR HAROUN

You are the eldest son of Ali and Nuria Haroun. You work as a bus driver for the Israeli-owned Upper Galilee Tours, Ltd., Company.

Your experience of Europeans and Americans on the bus you drive has upset you. You don't understand how the tour guides put up with it. The women seem loud, vulgar, and demanding. Your own wife, on the other hand, is quiet, loyal, and affectionate. She limits herself to cooking and raising children.

You think it would be unseemly for Fawzia to receive more education than any of her brothers. You think it would be best for her and for everyone else if she were like your wife.

AMIR HAROUN

You are Fawzia's brother and are twenty-three years old. You are a tank commander in the Israeli army. You have met Israeli and westernized Arab women outside Fetya. They seem to maintain appropriate roles while pursuing careers. Your own wife has only an elementary school education, which seems sufficient. Still, you are proud of Fawzia's ambitions.

You are also proud of the family's honor and hope that it will not be threatened by the issue.

DAOUD HAROUN

You are Fawzia's twenty-one-year-old brother. You are studying to be a traditional religious leader. Preparation for the role is very demanding. You have made a total commitment of yourself to it. Although religious feeling is very strong in Fetya, you are worried about the growing secularism in the community. You feel that women going on to higher education is likely to lead to less respect for Druze social and religious traditions.

The idea of your own sister behaving like a "liberated" Israeli woman is very upsetting. You must present your comments to her both as a brother and as a member of the traditional religious leadership.

NAVA HAROUN

You are a cousin of Fawzia, but you live in Beirut, Lebanon. As a city girl, you were fully educated. You were one of the few Druze girls educated at the American University in Beirut. There is a lot of violence now in Lebanon, so your husband is moving your family to Haifa, a city in Israel.

When you visited Fawzia's family for a wedding last year, you were impressed by your cousin's obvious intelligence. You encouraged her to consider college and would like her to go. You think it would help bring desirable modern ideas to the mountain people.

Saamia Haroun

You are Fawzia's older sister. You are married to a Fetya man who drives a truck for an Israeli construction company. You have two children and are at home taking care of them.

You have always liked Fawzia, and you want her to be happy. You are very close to your father. You are pleased that he was able to arrange a marriage for you with a man from your own village. (Druze brides go to live in the village of the husband's family.) You feel that a lot of the happiness in your own life comes from its traditional ways. But you are not sure whether Fawzia could be happy with a traditional woman's life.

Selah Haroun

You are a twenty-five-year-old brother of Fawzia. You work installing telephone equipment in the mountain towns with a mixed group of Israelis, Arabs, and Druze.

You enjoy Israelis and have some pleasant friendships among them. But you disapprove of what you see of westernized family life on television. Women seek divorce from husbands they don't like. Children move away when they grow up and do not spend much time with their parents.

You think Fawzia is a good daughter and sister. But you worry about how an Israeli college would change her.

ACHMED BADOUR

You are one of the elders of the village of Fetya. You are also a personal friend of Yusuf Haroun, the grandfather of the girl who wants to go to college. You are one of the men who led the village through the difficult period when Israel declared its independence. Battles with the Syrian army raged in the hills around Fetya.

The people of Fetya survived that difficult period with their village unharmed and their lands intact. The reason, you believe, is your villagers' strong feeling of community and loyalty to each other. You have seen nearby Arab villages that also survived well. But they then lost their lands when younger men readily gave in to Israeli pressure to sell. You must not allow that to happen in Fetya.

Once a few basic traditions are given up, how can the line be drawn? A family that is careless about a daughter's honor will be careless about holding on to the land.

You must urge your friend Yusuf not to allow his granddaughter to challenge traditions.

HASSAN MABDAN

You are a prominent leader of the Druze community of Bet Ja'an. Some years ago you arranged a wedding match with Ali Haroun for his daughter Fawzia to marry your son Jamal. The youngsters have been pleased with the match, and Fawzia seems to be a fine girl. Now you have heard that she wants to go to college.

When Fawzia marries your son, they will live in Bet Ja'an. Your family has earned great honor and prestige in this village, where leadership is traditional. The village elders would be horrified at the idea of a Druze woman going away from her village to an Israeli college. It would mean dishonor for her and for all her relatives.

You must make your feelings on this known to your son and to the Haroun family.

URI BEN-SHEM

You have been assigned to the Arab Education Department in Israel's Ministry of Education and Culture. As a Jew, you are sensitive to the charge that Israeli Arabs have not been given adequate educational opportunities.

You feel that more college-educated teachers are needed to upgrade Arab education in general and Druze education in particular. You know that many Druze men prefer a more active life than that of a teacher. So you are interested in encouraging the education of women. Fawzia Haroun could be the first of a new generation of well-educated Druze women.

MARYAM RANMANI

You are a Christian Arab girl whose father manages the regional bank in Fetya. You are not one of Fawzia's closest friends; they are all Druze girls. However, you have always liked Fawzia and are sure she would be a good companion in college. It is also a long bus ride to Haifa. It would be nice to take it every day with a fellow student.

You know enough about the Druze people to understand their traditions, although your parents moved here ten years ago from Nazareth. As a minority group member in Fetya, you would like to see more interaction between the different peoples.

JAMAL MABDAN

You are a young man from the Druze community of Bet Ja'an. Some years ago your father worked out the arrangements with Ali Haroun for you to marry Fawzia. The wedding is scheduled to take place in a few years. By then you will have completed a training program for agricultural technicians you are about to begin.

You want to learn modern farming techniques in order to improve the productivity of Druze farms. Modern technology interests you, and "modern thinking" seems to go with it. You think it would be fine for your wife to have a complete education. But you know it would upset your father, whom you deeply respect.

BIBLIOGRAPHY

Al-Qazzaz, Ayad, Ruth Afifi, and Audrey Shabbas. *Arab World Notebook: Secondary School Level*. Berkeley, CA: NAJDA, 1989.

Beck, Lois, and Nikki Keddie, eds. *Women in the Muslim World*. Cambridge, MA: Harvard University Press, 1978.

Ben-Dor, Gabriel. *The Druzes in Israel: A Political Study*. New York: The Magnes Press, 1979.

Betts, Robert B. *The Druze*. New Haven: Yale University Press, 1988.

Dana, Nissim. *The Druze: A Religious Community in Transition*. Jerusalem: Turtledove Press, 1977.

Fernea, Elizabeth W., and Basima Bezirgan, eds. *Middle Eastern Muslim Women Speak*. Austin: University of Texas Press, 1977.

GEM, eds. *Women in the Middle East*. Hudson, WI: GEM Publications, 1988.

Moghadam, Valentine. *Modernizing Women: Gender and Social Change in the Middle East*. Boulder, CO: Lynne Riener, 1993.

Nydell, Margaret. *Understanding Arabs*. Yarmouth, ME: Intercultural Press, 1987.

Parssinen, Catherine. "The Changing Role of Women," in *King Faisal and the Modernization of Saudi Arabia*, edited by Willard A. Beling. London: Croon Helm, 1980.

Pearson, Robert, ed. *Through Middle Eastern Eyes*. New York: CITE, 1992.

Prothro, Edwin T. *Changing Family Patterns in the Arab East*. Syracuse: Syracuse University Press, 1974.

Tucker, Judith, ed. *Arab Women: Old Boundaries, New Frontiers*. Bloomington, IN: Indiana University Press, 1993.

UNESCO Editorial Staff. *Social Science Research and Women in the Arab World*. London: L Frances Pinter, 1984.

AFRICA SOUTH OF THE SAHARA

Nationalism Versus Tribal Loyalties

BACKGROUND

The conflict between tribal and national loyalties has been a continuing difficulty for a number of African nations. Loyalties based on a common political organization—particularly when the boundaries of the political entity reflect European arrangements rather than local demography—are hard to establish in an area where postcolonial political independence is generally less than twenty years old.

It is important first to understand that the term *tribe* has usually been misused in European and American reports on Africa. *Tribe* has usually connoted a lower level of civilization; the term *tribesmen* usually implies people who are "primitive." Since these indications are false as well as demeaning, it would be better to use some other term connoting ethnic societies. Unfortunately, the academic as well as journalistic materials available to the class still use *tribe* for African peoples, so we shall also utilize it. But it is important for the class first to hold a discussion to clarify the images just discussed.

Tribal loyalties are powerful, and in many cases were intentionally promoted during the colonial era by imperialist rulers who feared unity among the colonized peoples. Because there were few public welfare institutions to care for the sick, the poor, and the injured in the colonial era, support systems based on kinship were enforced. With independence, African nations are offering national welfare systems. But with limited resources to support the official systems, nations still see people relying on kinship rather than citizenship.

The general topic of loyalty to ethnic or kinship groups as a challenge to national unity is important in many parts of the world, particularly in Asia, and can be discussed in those contexts.

Historical Note:

As of this writing, there were some efforts to convert Zimbabwe to a single-party state. If this change has in fact taken effect when you are using this case, you may want to reset the simulation to a different, multiparty nation.

SCENARIO

Josiah Ndema and Okot Bende are students at the University of Zimbabwe at Harare. They will soon be graduating and going into separate careers. The two men are members of the same tribe and have known each other for many years. As they think ahead to their future careers, they find themselves interested in the future of their nation.

Zimbabwe only achieved full independence in 1980. Black political systems are still evolving. In the first years of freedom, political organizations grew out of the guerrilla movements. These had arisen to overthrow the white minority government, which had ruled since 1965 and retained the British colonial name of Rhodesia. Different guerrilla organizations built their followings around different tribes. But there were people from more than one tribe in each group.

Josiah and Okot represent the new generation of leaders who are coming of age in many African nations. With independence no longer in doubt, permanent political patterns are being developed. Ways of establishing loyalties compatible with a nation must be found. At the same time, other loyalties that have guided these societies for centuries cannot be ignored.

Josiah and Okot have different ideas about what type of political party is best for their country. They are planning to ask friends, relatives, and acquaintances for their opinions on the subject.

JOSIAH NDEMA

You are very interested in politics. You expect you will be a political activist no matter what profession you choose. As a student of modern history, you have taken a special interest in Africa and have read a lot about other African nations. You know that they have chosen a variety of political systems, from rigid dictatorship to open democracy. You hope that open democracy will be the long-term pattern for Zimbabwe.

You feel that the best prospects for democracy lie in political parties with a national base. All tribes and ethnic groups should be represented in all the major parties. Then no area or tribe will feel excluded by a victory of any political party. Everyone will have a stake in the nation no matter which party wins.

OKOT BENDE

You admire the idealism of your friend Josiah. But you wonder about his realism. In a new country, leaders have to develop strong followings that will support them in difficult times. This means counting on the support of people who are already likely to be in one's favor—for example, people from the same tribe.

In the future the nation will be long established. There will be no doubts about the commitment of the government to consider everyone's needs. Perhaps then people will no longer require the security of a political group based on their own tribe. Until that time, it may be best to stick with those who share the same background.

KAFI BARUMBI

You are a leader of the tribal activists. Although your tribe is a minority of all the people of Zimbabwe, it is one of the largest tribes in the country. By identifying with one political party, your tribe could have a lot of influence in the government. No official would want to ignore a group that is so well organized and is directly involved in politics. Your tribal party could get together with one or two other parties and represent a majority of the country.

You want to persuade Josiah and others to stick with the idea of a tribally based party as the key to influence.

NANDI ARANDO

As a woman student, you are especially interested in changing certain traditions. Most women in your country still have limited opportunities, especially in the rural areas where most people live. You want to be sure the government increases opportunities for women. It must discard the limits on women's choices that have been kept in place by old traditions.

You know that tribal loyalties are much stronger in the countryside than in the towns. So tribally based parties would be more likely to preserve the old-fashioned ideas of the country people. That would mean less interest in educating women and, therefore, fewer careers open to them.

You will speak out against building political parties around tribes.

ABIOSEH MURIANI

You are a journalist and have traveled a good deal in many parts of Africa. You are concerned about the civil wars and rioting that occurred in the early years of a number of African nations. You believe that these nations did not have a firmly enough established commitment to national unity. You do not want such things to happen to Zimbabwe.

You believe people must limit the loyalties that they have given to their tribes and local communities for so long. Until then, national unity will not be fully secure. If each tribe has its own political party, the national government will think of what is best for the most powerful tribes. It will fail to consider what is best for the entire nation.

You are particularly interested in the new generation of educated young people. You want to persuade them to place national interests ahead of tribal traditions and to organize political movements across tribal lines.

BIRAGO NDEMA

You are Josiah's uncle. You still live in the small country village that has been the home of the Ndemas for generations. When Josiah went away to the university, you were worried. You feared he would forget many important traditions of his family and his tribe.

Now your friends tell you Josiah is interested in politics; but wants to support a political party not based on tribal membership. You want to persuade Josiah to change his ideas.

You remember the difficult times during the rebellion against the white dictatorship of Rhodesia. Although you were not personally involved, there was a lot of fighting not far from your village. You survived because you were always able to ask any member of your tribe to protect you. Such loyalty cannot be found in political parties that have not been tested in crisis. It is best to stay close to one's own tribe, and you will remind Josiah of that.

ABENA THOLE

You are a woman who has been educated in the United States. You have returned to Zimbabwe, your homeland, to train local nurses. Your years in the United States showed you how the American system works. You want to share some of the ideas you picked up.

You believe the United States gained much of its power because of a united national government. Germans, French, Italians, and others have fought many wars against each other in Europe. Nevertheless, Americans have organized one national government that includes people who were once Germans, French, Italians, and others.

To you, a tribal political party would be like an "Irishmen's Party" or a "Jewish Party" in America. It would be bound to fail, and it would only divide the country.

CAMARA ATSWEYO

You are a veteran guerrilla fighter who was active in the war for Zimbabwe's independence. Now you are worried about tribal leaders who want to keep their own tribes in separate political parties. You are sure that such a system would produce weak governments.

You fought to guarantee the freedom of all the people of Zimbabwe. You did not want to create a system in which important decisions could only be made by deals among separate tribal organizations. The government, and the parties that create it, must represent people from all kinds of tribes.

European imperialists kept Africans weak by keeping them divided. To you, returning to tribal loyalties mimics this tactic. You want to convince Okot that his friend Josiah has the best approach for a strong, free country.

KAMUZU TUNDE

You are a village elder and leader of a group dedicated to resisting many of the recent changes in Zimbabwe. You are deeply committed to the old tribally and regionally based system. You oppose the development of a strong national government.

You are suspicious of all these changes. The old ways looked good to you. If someone was charged with a crime, the case was handled by the village elders. They knew the accused and the accuser. Their judgment took into account personal situations as well as the special traditions of the local people. Judges and police who are assigned by a central government want to handle all cases the same way. They have no respect for special tribal traditions.

You want to convince Josiah to abandon the idea of a political system that is not based on tribal loyalties.

SARAH WARNO

You are a woman student at the university and are engaged to marry Josiah Ndema. You agree with his belief in the importance of national loyalties, and not only because he is your fiancé.

You have greatly enjoyed the mixture at the university of students from many tribes. Some of them have become your best friends. But you know you could not have gotten friendly with people from other tribes in your home village.

You would like all of Zimbabwe to be like the university. Here, all kinds of people can get to know each other and work together on exciting projects. Just look at the soccer team—there is one example of bringing together talents that might never otherwise have been shared.

You will support Josiah and those who are speaking in favor of more national unity.

BIBLIOGRAPHY

Burke, Fred, ed., *Africa: Selected Readings*. Boston: Houghton Mifflin, 1974.

Clark, Leon, ed. *Through African Eyes: Cultures in Change*. New York: Praeger, 1991.

Cobb, Charles E. "After Rhodesia, Zimbabwe." *National Geographic*, November 1981.

Harden, Blaine. *Africa: Dispatches from a Fragile Continent*. New York: Norton, 1990.

Hollings, Jill. *African Nationalism*. New York: Day, 1972.

Knight, Virginia. "Zimbabwe: The Politics of Reform." *Current History*, May 1992.

Kpatinde, Francis. "Jaded Students." *Jeune Afrique*, reprinted in *World Press Review*, December 1991.

Kraus, John. "Building Democracy in Africa." *Current History*, May 1991.

Lessing, Doris. *African Laughter: Four Visits to Zimbabwe*. New York: Harper, 1992.

Samkange, Stanlake, and Tommie Marie Samkange. *Hunhuism or Ubuntuism: A Zimbabwean Indigenous Philosophy*. Harare: Graham, 1980.

Stoneman, Colin. *Zimbabwe's Inheritance*. New York: St. Martin, 1982.

Vambe, Lawrence. *From Rhodesia to Zimbabwe*. Pittsburgh: University of Pittsburgh Press, 1976.

Wiley, Marylee. "Teaching About Africa." *Social Education*, December 1982.

SOUTH AMERICA

Urbanization Versus Village Life

BACKGROUND

Urbanization was one of the most important and dramatic phenomena in the cultural changes that affected Europe and the United States in the nineteenth century. Today it is one of the dominant forces for change in most of the Third World. Among the most spectacular examples are the metropolitan centers of Latin America. Mexico City, Rio de Janeiro, Bogotá, and other cities are literally growing faster than can be recorded.

Your students should realize that the style of the situation in this simulation is a reflection of the specifics of a Latin American democracy. However, the issues would be virtually the same in many parts of the Third World. You would only have to add in such variables as available transportation and degree of movement allowed by authoritarian governments to apply this case to another culture being explored.

Other issues you might consider include the impact of urbanization on traditional rural families after they have moved to the city. These are socially disruptive forces that can radically affect the structure of the family. We have not dealt much with this issue in our simulation because it would be unrealistic for a peasant family to have extensive insight into the topic. However, there are good sources for discussing the problem in the bibliography for this section.

Scenario

Juan and Carmen Cordona moved to Bogotá a few years ago from the poor village of Gireto. Juan had worked with his family on his father's farm there. But the farm was too small to support a large family, and the soil was not really very productive. The Cordonas had hoped to find something better in the city.

They still live in a hillside shack that they put together for "temporary" quarters when they arrived. Juan's limited education has kept him from getting steady work in a city with so many unskilled workers. Carmen finds it hard to raise their six children in the *barriada* (shantytown). Regular sources of water and sanitation are lacking.

Juan's brother Miguel is in Bogotá visiting the Cordonas. When he sees the squalor of their shanty, he suggests they return with him to the village. He knows someone with a truck who will be leaving Bogotá soon. Juan and Carmen have to decide whether to use the opportunity to move back to the old home.

ANTONIO PALMARES

You are a friend of Juan Cordona. Like the Cordonas, you grew up in a small village and moved to Bogotá. You have lived in the city for ten years and would never leave. Unlike the Cordonas, your family was not desperately poor in the farm village. But you found life in a little mountain town just too dull.

You don't have much education, so you have never made much money. What really interests you in Bogotá is not the chance for more income, but the chance for more activity. There are so many things to see and do in a great city like this! In your old village, no one ever went anywhere except to the fields and their homes. At night, everyone went to bed early; there was nothing else to do. Not so in the big city, however.

You like the Cordonas and want to persuade them to stay in Bogotá.

JUAN CORDONA

You are thirty years old and have lived in Bogotá for five years. Right now, you have no regular job. You have watched the construction of a new warehouse nearby and hope you can get a job there when it opens. But many other men may also expect to apply for jobs there.

You remember being just as poor when you lived in Gireto. In the village, however, you never really worried about food. Somehow, there was always enough for everyone to eat. And there were many relatives and close friends there to help whenever someone was sick or other problems came. But there was only a small elementary school, and it was a long walk in the mountains to get there. There was no nearby high school. The nearest doctor was very far away. Your nephew Miguelito died when no doctor could be found in time to help him.

Life in the city seems hard and uncertain. But there are possibilities, especially for the children.

Carmen Cordona

You are twenty-eight years old and have lived in Bogotá for five years. Raising six children in the hillside shantytown has been very difficult. Your husband has only been able to get temporary, unskilled jobs. You know that his lack of education prevents his ever getting a good permanent job.

You know that Juan, your husband, is tempted by his brother's offer to get your family moved back to your home village of Gireto. But you do not think this would be a good idea. There was always poverty in Gireto. Basic food and friendly relatives were always available. However, there seemed to be no way to improve your lives in that limited village.

Your children are going to school now. Some of them will go to high school—something not available in Gireto. True, the older children may have to go to work before finishing school. Yet they will still have much more education and better opportunities than in the village.

Your own life seems more interesting here. You have made friends with some neighborhood women. You enjoy hearing them tell about parts of Colombia that you have never seen.

You will try to persuade Juan to stay in Bogotá.

Luisa Sanchez

You are the mother of Carmen Cordona. You live in the village of Gireto and have never been to Bogotá.

You are excited at the news that your daughter and her family may return to the village. It would be nice to have her and your grandchildren nearby so you could see each other easily.

But you know there are no real opportunities for the grandchildren in the village. The schools are very limited. There are few jobs to look forward to when they grow up. You are not sure what advice to send to your daughter.

Maria Simona

You are the sister of Carmen Cordona. You still live in the village of Gireto, but you have visited the Cordonas in Bogotá. Your husband's family, the Simonas, have always lived in Gireto. You have known your husband since you were both very young. Your parents arranged the marriage, for both families knew each other well.

You have heard that marriages are different in the city. Girls meet young men at work or in the streets, and they start going out together. Weddings result in which the parents have not been consulted and little is known about the groom's family.

You think that such behavior is dangerous. You will warn your sister to return to Gireto before her daughters start to behave in ways of which you disapprove.

Alfredo Gomez

You are a public health planner for the government of Colombia. Your studies show that people are moving into the cities faster than public services can be provided. Places like Bogotá cannot absorb the rural people who are swarming into the urban centers.

Because of the swift growth, many centers get out of control. People move into an area before any sewers can be built. Disease soon sweeps through the neighborhood. People who have no water pipes get water from other places, leaving those other faucets to run all day. Then there is not enough to keep the water flowing for everybody.

Somehow, many people must be moved out of the overcrowded cities to get things back under control. You will try to convince the Cordonas to move back to the countryside.

JOSE PARNADO

You are a political organizer in the Cordona's Bogotá neighborhood. Although you are not a close friend of the family, they are like many other families in the area. You do know them well enough to help. You think they should stay in Bogotá.

You know how poor some of the facilities in the neighborhood are, such as schools and medical care. But you also know that these facilities are much worse in the mountain villages. It seems much more realistic to work on programs in the cities. There, housing is not so thinly spread out and changes are not so strongly resisted.

You will suggest to the Cordonas the advantages of staying in the city.

MIGUEL CORDONA

You are Juan's older brother. You are upset by the neighborhood where your brother lives. The poverty is not so disturbing, because you are used to poverty in your village. But people's lives seem too depressing in Bogotá.

You are especially upset by all the crime you hear about in the city. Back in Gireto, no one ever has anything stolen, and doors have no locks on them. The idea that one of your own neighbors might steal from you seems a dreadful idea. That alone is a good reason to leave the city and move back to Gireto. You will tell your brother this.

Alfredo Cordona

You are the twelve-year-old son of Juan and Carmen. You remember something of life in the village and do not want to go back there. All the children seemed just to hang around with nothing to do. Some of them, including you, went to school, but everyone knew they would have no education beyond elementary school.

Now you are going to a much better school and are doing well there. You are a good student. Your teachers have said you might someday even win a scholarship to college.

The family's moving back to the village would mean the end of your education.

Hernando Cordona

You are thirteen years old and are the oldest son of Juan and Carmen. Unlike your brother Alfredo, you are not a very good student. You have dropped out of school. When you finished the elementary grades, you found that the secondary school was a long walk from home. And there were so many distractions on the way there!

You soon found it was more fun to leave school and hang around with a group of boys who like to spend their time at the bus station. Your group has had some fights with other boys. Sometimes the police have chased you away from the bus station for causing disturbances. But it is an exciting way of life.

You remember a little of village life. You also hear about life in the rural villages from people around the bus station. It sounds dull and hopeless. You are upset at the idea of your family's considering a return to Gireto.

BIBLIOGRAPHY

Borrini, G. "Miuda's World: Squatter Settlement." *UNESCO Courier*, September 1992.

De la Haba, Louis. "Mexico, the City that Founded a Nation." *National Geographic*, May 1973.

Dinges, John. "Bogotá: Anatomy of a Third World City." *Urban Edge*, October 1984.

Dubois, Victor D. "City Lights: the Urbanization Process in Abidjan," Hanover, NH: American Universities Field Staff, 1970.

Fox, Robert W. "The World's Urban Explosion." *National Geographic*, August 1984.

Lewis, Oscar. *Five Families: Mexican Case Studies in the Culture of Poverty.* New York: Basic Books, 1959.

McDowell, Bart. "Mexico City: An Alarming Giant." *National Geographic*, August 1984.

Mangin, William. "Urbanization: Case Study in Peru." *Architectural Design*, August 1963.

Patch, Richard W. "Life in a 'Callejon': A Case Study of Urban Disorganization." Hanover, NH: American Universities Field Staff, 1970.

Veslind, Priit J. "Brazil: Moment of Promise and Pain." *National Geographic,* March 1987.

Whiteford, Andrew H. *Two Cities of Latin America.* New York: Doubleday, 1964.

CENTRAL AMERICA

Reform or Revolution?

BACKGROUND

The current political crises in Central America draw upon such an interweaving of economic, social, political, and even international issues that this simulation leaves a great many points to explore further. We have chosen El Salvador because at the time of this writing it seemed to combine some key ingredients—ongoing violence, extremism of both right and left, major elements of a functioning democracy, difficulty in proving responsibility for political crimes, and general agreement that the present situation has to be changed. Obviously, the situation may have altered by the time this simulation is used in class. You can then decide whether to leave the case as written, to indicate the background leading to later developments, to change the country to another Central American republic, or to change the roles to reflect current realities in El Salvador.

This simulation was written to highlight attitudes being expressed in the many parts of Central America. However, the basic issue—whether to trust in democratic processes or to use organized violence as an instrument of change—is a recurring concern in many parts of the world, from Northern Ireland to Sri Lanka. To adapt the simulation for other critical areas, students need only research current newspaper or magazine reports to convert the relative positions—moderates and extremists—to the specifics of crises elsewhere.

SCENARIO

El Salvador has been the scene of continuous political upheaval and great violence through the 1980's. A majority of its people want basic changes in the country. However, they disagree on the direction and on the swiftness of change.

Alicia Gomez, Alberto Carreras, and Luis Molnaro are college students in San Salvador, the capital city of El Salvador. They are all critical of what has been happening in their country. But they differ on what should be done about it.

Alicia thinks the only hope is a violent revolution. She therefore supports the guerrillas who have been attacking government forces in the countryside.

Alberto believes that the guerrillas are puppets of Cuba and Nicaragua, which he considers Communist regimes. He thinks force can only be opposed by force. He supports right-wing leaders who want a stronger military and whatever force is necessary.

Luis thinks that considerable changes are needed. However, he is afraid that the method of the guerrillas—bloody warfare—is not the right way. It can only lead to more bloodshed. He hopes for peaceful change.

So far, the students' "support" has only been conversation. Now they are interested in joining organized groups. But first they will try to convince their friends of their views.

ALICIA GOMEZ

You are a college student with a special interest in chemistry. But you have not paid so much attention to schoolwork lately. The political turmoil in your country cannot be ignored, and you find yourself heavily involved.

It seems to you that the situation requires an extreme solution. Poverty is so widespread, and the government seems so afraid of offending the wealthy privileged class. Only a total revolution can really change things.

Legal reforms and figuring out who the violators of civil rights are, proving it, and then punishing them are gradual changes. They will take years—if they happen at all. Meanwhile, abuses continue.

You want to convince your friends that the need is for immediate, swift, and extreme action. A few innocent people may suffer, but it is the only way to make real changes.

ALBERTO CARRERAS

You have been an average student, although you are fairly bright. You know you will inherit a successful family business, so you have not seen any need for working too hard in college.

Right now, you are worried more about politics than education. It seems to you that when guerrilla spokesmen are asked about their models for "reform," the model always turns out to be Cuba or the Sandanistas in Nicaragua. You consider both of those governments Communist dictatorships maintained by force.

The liberals are stupid to think that changes in the constitution or economic opportunities would satisfy the guerrillas. The only way to handle force is by force. That means giving more authority to the army and having it do whatever is necessary to wipe out the guerrilla movement.

You will warn your friends that they do not understand what is necessary. You will tell them they should support a powerful army that will prevent a Communist takeover.

LUIS MOLNARO

You used to be a good student, but lately your interest has been drawn more into politics than education. Your country is in a terrible crisis, and you cannot ignore it.

Reform is badly needed. Many people were arrested without warning when the generals controlled the government. The victims were denied their rights, and many of them were murdered. Other people were so terrified by the army's actions that they dared not criticize or question anything.

At the same time, the country has growing numbers of very poor people. Basic things like education, health care, and steady employment are not available to them.

A reform program was introduced in 1980, redistributing land and reforming finances. You believe this was an important first step. Other key reforms are needed, but they will only work if people accept careful democratic changes.

You will try to convince your friends that violence only forces people into extremes and prevents the changes that are necessary.

EMILIO COLON

You agree with Alicia that immediate total change is necessary. You have been spending time among the poor people in the countryside. Their misery is so great that many "reforms" are meaningless for them.

Ideas like freedom of the press are luxuries when people are at the mercy of a landowner who will not pay farm workers enough to support their families.

Reforms do not produce results fast enough. You want action now. The property of the wealthy and the middle class must be redistributed so that everyone will have a better share. Obviously, this can only be done by force.

You will warn your friends that a violent takeover is necessary.

CARLOTTA MONAGAS

You are a member of one of the wealthiest families in San Salvador. Your private collection of local art is well known. Displays of it have put you in touch with local students.

You are afraid that many students do not understand how serious the threat of the guerrilla movement could be. It seems to you that the guerrillas are really working for foreign troublemakers. Support from foreign governments is what has kept the guerrillas going for so long.

Before all the violence began, you used to go into the mountains for picnics and sightseeing. When you stopped in local villages, people treated you with respect. They seemed sincerely grateful when you gave them gifts for carrying the items you needed.

The fact that people from such areas may now be supporting guerrillas must mean that foreign agitators have been disturbing them. Crushing the guerrilla movement would really mean driving a foreign influence out of El Salvador.

You will explain to the students why the army must be given unrestricted power to stamp out the guerrillas.

Lorenza Portillo

You are a schoolteacher from a town outside San Salvador. This year, you are at the university taking new courses, and you have gotten to know the students. You feel that many of them do not understand what it is like in the countryside. You have to explain it to them.

The peasants have been living in constant terror. Sometimes guerrillas come into the villages, urging the people to join in the struggle to overthrow the government. Sometimes the guerrillas use force themselves, threatening the lives of people who do not cooperate. Then army troops come to the village and accuse people of supporting the guerrillas. The accused people, many of them innocent, are arrested. Some have never been seen again.

You believe the country's only hope is an elected government that really cares about the people. Such a government would both stop the guerrillas and punish the military officers who have encouraged many murders. Politicians must convince the public that they really want to make people's lives better and to control extremists on both sides.

You will support Luis Molnaro and urge other students to go along with him.

RAFAEL VEGA

You have recently returned to the university in San Salvador from a long visit with relatives in Mexico. Actually, you did not stay long in Mexico but spent most of your time in Cuba. You had to do this secretly because the El Salvador security forces might arrest someone who had made a long visit in Cuba.

You were very impressed by what you saw in Cuba. Before you went there, you had heard the charges that Castro had taken away democracy and personal liberty. That seems to be true. But you also saw that Cuba had jobs for all, a huge education program, and a strong commitment to health facilities. People did not seem to lack food and a place to live.

You have decided that food, clothing, and housing are essential. Other things are optional. Perhaps when the essential needs have been met, democracy could be thought about. Until then, such a system is a luxury.

You will tell your friends that Cuba is the model to follow, and you will support Alicia Gomez.

OCTAVIO FURTADO

You are a student at the university, but you will have to leave before graduation. Your father was an army officer who has been killed in a guerrilla ambush. You will have to take over the affairs of your family.

To you, the liberals are hopelessly unrealistic. Their idea that a popularly supported government will solve problems by legal means is absurd. The guerrillas will continue to attack by using help from other countries. And people will support the guerrillas because they are afraid of them.

You think the solution is to make people more afraid of the government. Then they would not dare to help the guerrillas or to criticize seriously anything the government does.

You want the students to understand that nothing can be accomplished without order. And the army must be given total authority to create order.

FATHER LOPEZ

You are a Roman Catholic priest. Although your current assignment is to be a chaplain at the university, you have been a parish priest in the countryside and know El Salvador very well.

You are upset that many people do not realize how much suffering the common people have endured. For years, most of their taxes went to support the privileges of the ruling generals and their wealthy friends. Finally, in 1980, real reforms were begun. But unstable governments and police terror have prevented any real improvement in people's lives. "Death squads" have murdered people, including priests and nuns, who tried to help the poor people.

You deeply believe that violence is *NOT* the answer. Violence by the military will not stop the people's basic need for justice. And violence by guerrillas will not convince the army to stop interfering with the government.

You want the students to support a program of peace and justice. The wealthy few will give up their privileges and everyone will back a government committed to the will of the people.

BIBLIOGRAPHY

Ania, J. "El Salvador's Uneasy Truce." *World Press Review,* November 1992.

Baylora, Enrique. *El Salvador in Transition.* Chapel Hill: University of North Carolina Press, 1982.

————"The Persistent Conflict in El Salvador." *Current History,* March 1991.

Cheney, Glenn A. *El Salvador: Country in Crisis.* New York: Franklin Watts, 1984.

————. *Revolution in Central America.* New York: Franklin Watts, 1984.

Colburn, Forrest D. "The Fading of the Revolutionary Era in Central America." *Current History,* February 1992.

Dominguez, Jorge, and Marc Lindenburg. *Central America: Current Crisis and Future Prospects.* New York: Foreign Policy Association, 1985.

Gettleman, Marvin, ed. *El Salvador: Central America in the New Cold War.* New York: Grove Press, 1981.

Wesson, Robert. *U.S. Influences in Latin America in the 1980's.* New York: Praeger, 1982.

Wiarde, Howard J. *Politics and Social Change in Latin America.* Amherst: University of Massachusetts Press, 1974.

Woodward, Ralph L. *Central America: A Nation Divided.* New York: Oxford University Press, 1976.

CANADA

A National or Local Language?

BACKGROUND

In the past twenty years there has been a marked increase in separatist movements by ethnic minorities in many parts of the world. Some of these groups—e.g., the Basques in Spain, the Sikhs in India—have developed violent elements who have resorted to terrorist acts to promote their cause. Others—e.g., the Kurds in Iran, the Moluccans in Indonesia—have from time to time erupted into open warfare. Still others have not reached final agreement on their ultimate goals but are determined to turn their ethnic uniqueness from a handicap into an advantage. The French-speaking people of Canada are in this last category.

Although Francophone people make up only 29 percent of Canada's population (which is 45 percent British and 23 percent other European), they are the dominant majority of Quebec and a major force in other eastern provinces. As French resentment of the Anglophone majority grew, the separatist cause grew, especially in Quebec. In 1976 their organization, the Parti Quebecois, won control of the provincial government. Not satisfied with the national bilingual policy of Canada, Quebec has made itself a French-speaking province, with the kind of results that are explored in this simulation.

In thinking about wider application of these issues, students may also consider bilingual policies in American communities with large non-English-speaking minorities. If this topic has local significance, the class should consider bringing in spokespersons from the community or the school system with direct involvement in the issue.

SCENARIO

Adele Lorisse and Jean-Pierre Moneau are the newly chosen editors of a magazine to be published in the Province of Quebec. The publishers are investors who have decided not to get involved in the magazine's editorial policies. It will be up to the editors to select their own positions.

Because the magazine may have some influence, many people are approaching the editors with their opinions. They want the magazine to take an early stand on the question of how far Quebec should go in separating itself from the rest of Canada.

Most of the interest in pulling back from Canadian national identity has come from the province's French-speaking population. It forms the large majority of Quebec's people. English-speaking Canadians have always dominated the country's culture and economy. In the last twenty years, French-speaking Canadians' resentment of this situation has increased dramatically.

In 1976 Quebec came under the control of the Parti Quebecois. It put through a program severely restricting the use of English and requiring the use of French as the language of education, business, and public activity in the province. English-speaking citizens now claim to be suffering from discrimination.

The editors are ready to hear different views.

ADELE LORISSE

You are a native of Quebec City and have spent most of your professional career there. You come from a French-speaking family, but you speak English without an accent.

Your family have always been strong supporters of French-Canadian culture. They have raised you to share those values. In high school and college, you were active in groups that encouraged French language activities. As a writer you supported the Parti Quebecois—the local political party that has made French the only official language in the Province of Quebec.

As an editor, you will be in a position to further that cause. But you do not want to do so in a way that is unacceptable to your colleagues.

JEAN-PIERRE MONEAU

You come from a French-Canadian family in St. John, New Brunswick, on Canada's Atlantic coast. You are very much aware of the French-speaking culture: about 40 percent of New Brunswick's people are of French background. But the demand for a dominant French culture has never been as strong there as in Quebec. You are used to living in an English-speaking environment.

The Parti Acadien is the political party organized to create a separate French-speaking area in New Brunswick. It has never gotten much of a vote. The English majority has been cooperative in meeting the needs of the French community there.

You think that Canada's best path for national unity is through a national language. English is the logical choice, since it is the language of the great majority of Canadians. But there should be plenty of opportunity for French-speaking people to maintain their own culture in areas where they are the dominant group.

You hope that your colleagues on the magazine will agree with your position.

CLAUDE VACHON

You are a sales executive for a farm equipment company in Montreal, the largest city in the Province of Quebec. You started as a local salesman in small towns. You have worked your way up to being in charge of all sales throughout the province.

As a native French-speaking person, you have had a lot of success with farmers and farm equipment stores in Quebec. But now you are ready for a national position. You feel that the company considers people whose careers have been in Quebec to be not well prepared for dealing with people elsewhere in Canada.

You also know that the company would never consider moving any of the main offices to Montreal. This would be too limiting for the executives, who come from all over the rest of Canada.

You have been asked to take out ads in the new magazine. Before you do, you want to talk to the editors and suggest that they support a less narrowly French point of view.

DIANA WILSON

You are an employee of the Bank of Montreal. You have been doing well as an officer in the loan department. You learned Canadian French in high school and built on that to become quite at ease with the language. Your success in the banking field has enabled you to buy an apartment for your parents, who are retired and would like to live near you.

However, your parents speak only English and have never lived in a French-speaking city. They are hesitant about moving to a place where everyday signs and important notices may only be in French. They feel it is like visiting a foreign country, although they are Canadian born.

You believe your parents' fears demonstrate the dangers of overemphasizing cultural differences. You think it would be better if all parts of Canada emphasized the ways in which they are alike.

You have friends at the new magazine and will tell them how you feel.

BORIS KANCHENKO

You are a wealthy oil company president. You made a great fortune developing oil fields in the Province of Alberta, in western Canada. You have now opened offices in Quebec. You plan to explore for possible oil and gas fields in the northern part of that province.

You resent the Quebec government's insistence on its own local language, French. Actually, your own native language is Ukrainian. Your family came to Canada as refugees from World War II, and you learned English as an immigrant. But you don't speak French very well.

It seems ridiculous to you for someone to learn a special language for each part of Canada. You would not require French speakers to learn Ukrainian to be able to work in the part of Alberta where a number of Ukrainian refugees settled.

Before helping the new magazine, you want to get the editors to drop any support for French language programs.

JACQUES BOUDREAU

You are a politician—a member of Canada's House of Commons. You are a member of the Liberal party and have been described as one of the party's rising stars. The Liberal party represents the nationally oriented politicians of Quebec. The Parti Quebecois represents the locally oriented leaders.

You are interested in major issues affecting all of Canada. That is why you are in the House of Commons. You hope some day to be in the cabinet, or even prime minister. But you are afraid that people elsewhere in Canada may feel that a French-speaking politician from Quebec is too out of touch with the needs of the rest of the country.

You want to convince the magazine editors and other public leaders that Quebec should emphasize cooperation with the rest of Canada instead of a local French orientation.

MONIQUE FAVAUX

You are a filmmaker. Your studio is in Ottawa, in the English-speaking Province of Ontario. Right now you are visiting your family and friends in Quebec, where you grew up. You have heard about the new magazine and are interested in meeting the editors.

Your main fear centers around the United States. Your neighboring nation is very powerful, and very much like Canada in certain ways. So American ideas—and American movies and television—crowd out Canadian efforts in Canada. You think the best way to prevent this is to unite Canadian attitudes.

The media may divide itself among local interests—a French viewpoint for Quebec, an English one for Toronto, and so on. If so, there will not be anything powerful enough to stand up to American competition. The only hope for supporting Canadian media is to focus on things that are held in common by many Canadians.

You want to get the new magazine to emphasize national—mostly English-oriented—points of view.

MARIE BOUCHARD

You are a chemist in a laboratory near Montreal. You used to work for a big international company at its laboratory in Ontario in English-speaking Canada. There, other workers made fun of your French accent and the different way you pronounced certain words.

Now you have returned to the Province of Quebec. You are in a place where French is the official language. Here, the people with the English accents are the ones who seem to speak differently. You enjoy being able to relax and sound like everyone else. You think that requiring French as the official language for business was an excellent move by the Quebec government.

You are thrilled that your old college friend Adele is getting a chance to edit an important magazine. You will encourage her to use the magazine to promote a French point of view.

JEAN LECAULT

You are an artist. You were born in a small town in the Province of Quebec, and you still live there. Your paintings have been widely praised, and some of them have been sold for high prices. People wonder why you don't move to a big city, but you are happy to stay where you are.

You feel that your paintings are good because they show the real world around you. You portray the world of French-speaking farmers, workers, and business people. If you tried to paint something that was not part of your own life, it would not have this sense of reality.

You believe people do their best when they stay close to their roots. When people try to build a life among strangers, using a language they did not grow up with, they have to compromise. When they compromise, great achievements are not possible.

You are supposed to be interviewed for an article in the new magazine. You can use the chance to express your ideas about emphasizing special local attitudes.

CHARLOTTE JANET

You and your husband operate a bakery in Quebec City. Because of the exceptional quality of your bread and pastry, people come from all over to shop at your bakery. You have gotten to know important people like magazine editors because they are your customers.

You are a strong supporter of the Parti Quebecois and of those people who want to require an official French identity for the province. You believe that the special French flavor of the community is what makes it an exciting and special place.

What if all the economic power of English-speaking Canada were tied to the American economy? Canada might easily become just like part of the United States. French restaurants and bakeries would be replaced by frozen foods and McDonald's.

You want to keep Quebec interesting by keeping it French, and you will tell the editors so.

BIBLIOGRAPHY

Barlow, I.M. "Political Geography and Canada's National Unity Problem." *Journal of Geography*, December 1980.

Bercuson, David J., ed. *Canada and the Burden of Unity.* New York: New York University Press, 1977.

Brebner, J. Bartlett. *Canada: A Modern History.* Ann Arbor: University of Michigan Press, 1970.

Buchsbaum, H. "Canada's Culture War." *Scholastic Update* (Teacher Edition), November 1992.

Came, B. "A Grievance Upheld: The Case of B. McIntyre." *Maclean's*, May 1993.

Clift, Dominique. *Quebec: Nationalism in Crisis*. Montreal: McGill Queen's University Press, 1982.

Dion, Leon. *Quebec: The Unfinished Revolution*. Montreal: McGill Queen's University Press, 1974.

Finan, William, Jr., ed. "Canada: 1991." *Current History*, December 1991.

Holbrook, Sabra. *The French Founders of North America and Their Heritage.* New York: Atheneum, 1976.

Marin, Claude. *Quebec Versus Ottawa*. Toronto: University of Toronto Press, 1976.

Schwartz, Mildred. "Canadian Society: Trouble in Paradise." *Current History*, December 1991.

White, Peter T. "One Canada—or Two?"*National Geographic*, April 1977.

Wood, N. "Speaking Out: Francophones." *Maclean's*, April 1993.

UNITED STATES OF AMERICA

Multiculturalism and National Unity

Cultural Conflicts: Case Studies in a World of Change

BACKGROUND

In the 1990's the question of proper definition of our multicultural society has become a widely discussed issue for Americans. Although obviously a special concern for schools, the topic has also been receiving urgent attention in politics, law, entertainment, and the workplace, as well as the everyday exchanges of people.

The dramatic upsurge in immigration (legal and illegal) over the last decade has further stimulated discussion about the nature of a nation that has as its motto *E pluribus unum*—"From many, one." Is that "one" a random mixture of whatever ingredients are brought to it? Are these ingredients each modified by their contact with each other? Are they kept distinctly separate? Or are they all blended to the point where their separateness can no longer be identified?

The past concept of a "melting pot," wherein all origins were blended and an entirely new "American" character was created, is now widely criticized. But some of its defenders state that what they are supporting is a redefined melting pot—producing a national culture, but one that, unlike its earlier version, does not repress all traces of diverse ethnic origins.

There are related issues, such as the legal and political disputes over individual rights as distinct from group rights, that can also be explored. For example, an obvious issue for school concern is the curriculum itself: To what extent does it, and should it, reflect cultural diversity? At the same time, teachers may want to be selective about using roles that touch upon an issue that is of special sensitivity in a particular school.

SCENARIO

A growing school-age population has resulted in the building of a new high school for the Chicago suburb of Forest Glen. The faculty for the new Forest Glen South High School has been selected, and they are meeting in a week-long workshop to explore school plans. This session is charged with responsibility for defining cultural diversity for the school. The goal is to produce an official statement of the school's position on that subject.

The school district has made special efforts to recruit a faculty that reflects the cultural diversity of the community itself. Barbara Wilson has accepted the role of chairperson of the statement-writing team. She has asked her colleagues to present their own thoughts and to comment on each other's ideas.

BARBARA WILSON

You are chairperson of the English Department at Forest Glen South. When you came to the community twenty years ago, you were one of only a few African-American teachers in a faculty that was predominantly white Anglo-Saxon Protestant. You are now widely respected as a talented teacher whose circle of friends includes people from white and nonwhite backgrounds.

You are trying to pull together a statement that the group can agree on as a description of a culturally diverse school with which all students can identify. You know there is disagreement in the community as well as within the school about the goals of multicultural education.

You want to produce a statement that as many people as possible can accept, but it must be something that you can personally believe in.

LE'NIESSE HAZLETT

You are an African-American woman about to start on your second year of teaching. You were active in the Black Student Alliance in college, where you put in a lot of effort to get African-American history and culture courses added to the curriculum.

In your own early school years, you felt that the program offered little that you could identify with personally. Everything studied in school seemed to be about the culture of "dead white males." You do not want a similar program for Forest Glen South.

You want the new school to make a strong commitment to special curriculum offerings and other opportunities to celebrate African-American culture.

ELENA SONOMA

You are an art teacher at Forest Glen, and you commute from your home in Chicago. You and your husband have been active in Chicago politics, and you are proud of how much you have accomplished in getting your culturally mixed neighborhood to improve its appearance and local services.

You feel that your success in Chicago was achieved by getting people to care more about what they had in common—the neighborhood's own needs—than about the special claims of individual cultural groups, like your own Puerto Rican American affiliation.

You think the same ideas should apply to the school. People there should focus on what is shared—the school and its goals—rather than loyalty to some larger outside group—Mexican-Americans, African-Americans, etc.—that might simply divide the community.

RODOLFO HERNANDEZ

Your family moved to the Chicago area about fifty years ago; you grew up in a Mexican-American neighborhood. You are proud of your Chicano heritage and want to encourage Mexican-American students to adopt a strong Chicano identity.

You feel that special programs and courses on Mexico and Mexican-American history and traditions are necessary—both to support Chicano students and to create greater awareness among other students of this vital part of America.

You want the school's curriculum to include specific references to the celebration of Mexican-American culture.

CATHERINE SIKORSKI

You are a mathematics teacher whose family has lived in Chicago since your grandfather arrived as an immigrant from Poland in 1910. Although you now live in Forest Glen, you still maintain close ties to your relatives in Chicago.

You are disturbed by what you feel are the divisive tendencies of the emphasis on diversity. You were very upset to learn what has happened among your old Chicago neighbors. When you lived there, many of them were from Yugoslavia, and they enjoyed each other's company here. When Yugoslavia broke apart in the 1990's, neighbors with relatives in Serbia became enemies of neighbors with relatives in Croatia. Instead of enjoying an American neighborhood, they became enemies over things happening far away.

You think it is terrible that problems in Europe's Balkan area might "Balkanize" part of America. You oppose programs that emphasize the differences between people.

ALBERT BURTON

You have been teaching in the Forest Glen schools for thirty years. When you came here, the community was almost entirely Anglo-Saxon Protestant, and there was little interest in or welcoming of other cultural identities. As a result, you did not then mention the fact that your parents' original name was Bertonelli, and that they had shortened it after immigrating to the United States from Italy.

Although you now readily acknowledge your Italian-American background, you do not think that it is an important part of your public identity. Your parents saw to it that you spoke English without an accent. You and your family have not shown much interest in Italian customs and traditions, and you resent other people assuming that you will go into Chicago whenever there is an Italian festival there.

You think cultural background is a private matter. What should be emphasized is the common culture of all Americans.

HELEN MITCHELL

You are a science teacher at Forest Glen and have been in the school system for twenty years. You are not comfortable with the growing emphasis on different cultural identities.

You do not consider yourself a member of any particular cultural group. You and your husband's parents include Jewish, English, Greek, and German backgrounds. You have never been encouraged to think of any one of these groups as your special identity, and you do not want to.

When other kids ask your children what they "are," they answer "American." They do not like the suggestion that they should be choosing a particular cultural label. You believe that your own family represents a rejection of barriers between groups, and you oppose activities that might create such barriers or boundaries.

You want to be sure that the school's program emphasizes common values and de-emphasizes group differences.

MOUNIR ALI

Your family came from Pakistan twenty-five years ago, when your father received a fellowship to study physics at the Illinois Institute of Technology. They settled in Forest Glen; you are happy being a teacher in the town in which you grew up. Now there is a small but growing Muslim group in Forest Glen, mostly Pakistani and Iranian with some Arabs. As far as you know, you are the only Muslim teacher at the high school.

You are concerned about the apparent lack of sensitivity to Muslims shown by the community. Even the school casually accepts terms that exclude you—for example, referring to the Judeo-Christian tradition as an ethical guide. You hope that a statement on cultural diversity that specifically calls attention to the range of different groups and their special cultures will be helpful to your Muslim friends.

You want to convince your fellow teachers of the value of celebrating diversity.

BRUCE GOODMAN

You have been a guidance counselor at the old Forest Glen High School; you will be head of the guidance department at Forest Glen South. You have spent a lot of time talking individually and in groups with students who have had difficulty succeeding at the high school. You think that a strong multicultural program could help some of these youngsters.

Some minority students have expressed a bit of hostility to the school. They feel that the school seems to be run for the benefit of the "other kids"— well-to-do white students who are able to do well in history and English courses without ever having to learn about anyone else's culture. The Hispanic and African American students resent the fact that what is studied says so little about their own people's past and present.

You want to encourage the faculty to make a commitment to active celebration of minority cultures.

RICHARD KIM

You have just been hired to teach at Forest Glen South, but they have asked you to participate in the workshop because it was hard to get an Asian American teacher who was available for this week. You were not told that directly, but you heard informally that was how you got here.

You are quite proud of your college record. You do not want anyone to think that you were hired just because you were a member of a minority. You are also proud of your Korean background, but are not sure that you want to call attention to it in school.

You are well versed in Korean culture, primarily because your parents sent you to a Korean school on Saturdays in addition to the regular public school. That method of preserving a culture worked well for you, and you wonder why other groups cannot accept family responsibility for teaching the culture, and leave the public school to culturally neutral teaching.

BIBLIOGRAPHY

Acuna, Rodolfo. *Occupied America: A History of Chicanos* (3rd ed.). New York: Harper & Row, 1988.

Banks, James. "The Canon Debate, Knowledge Construction, and Multicultural Education." *Educational Researcher*, July 1993.

Banks, James, ed. *Multicultural Education: Issues and Perspectives*. Boston: Allyn & Bacon, 1989.

Bragaw, Don, and W. Scott Thomson, eds. *Multicultural Education: A Global Approach*. New York: The American Forum for Global Education, 1992.

D'Souza, Denesh. *Illiberal Education: The Politics of Race and Sex on Campus*. New York: Free Press, 1991.

Gates, Henry L., Jr. *Loose Canons: Notes on the Culture Wars*. New York: Oxford University Press, 1992.

Glazer, Nathan. "In Defense of Multiculturalism." *The New Republic*, September 1991.

Hirsch, E.D. Jr. *Cultural Literacy: What Every American Needs to Know*. Boston: Houghton Mifflin, 1987.

Ravitch, Diane. *Educating in a Multicultural World*. New York: The American Forum, 1992.

Schlesinger, Arthur M. *The Disuniting of America: Reflections on a Multicultural Society*. Knoxville, TN: Whittle, 1991.

Takaki, Ronald. *A Different Mirror: A History of Multicultural America*. Boston: Little Brown, 1993.

Viadero, Debra. "Battle over Multicultural Education Rises in Intensity." *Education Week*, November 28, 1990.

80 Activities to Make Basic Algebra Easier

Second Edition

by Robert S. Graflund

Grade Level: 6–Adult

| 5 | 6 | 7 | 8 | 9 | 10 | 11 | 12 | Adult |

Reading Level: 7

| 1 | 2 | 3 | 4 | 5 | 6 | 7 | 8 |

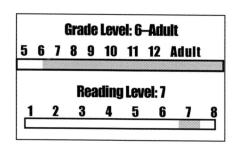

Number of Pages: 192

Copyright: 2001

**Type of Publication:
Reproducible Teacher Book**

J. WESTON
WALCH
PUBLISHER

321 Valley Street
P.O. Box 658
Portland, Maine 04104-0658

To place orders: 1-800-341-6094
To fax orders: 207-772-3105

www.walch.com

With this sourcebook of reproducible puzzles, activities, and practice problems, you can successfully reinforce first-year algebra skills with all your students. Secret codes, magic squares, cross-number puzzles, and other self-correcting devices provide stimulating and fun practice. Chapters cover basic equations, equations and inequalities with real numbers, polynomials, factoring, fractions, graphing, systems of linear equations, and rational and irrational numbers. In addition, hands-on "outdoor math" activities have been added.

See your students build a better understanding of basic algebraic skills and concepts. With *80 Activities to Make Basic Algebra Easier* you get:

- Short, easy-to-understand activities that use a variety of instructional methods and may be used as a means of concept introduction and/or independent or group learning

- Material that is revised to address the NCTM standards, packed with teaching tips and up-to-date calculator activities

- Teacher support including background information, practical teaching suggestions, a complete answer key, and more

80 Activities to Make Basic Algebra Easier

Second Edition

by Robert S. Graflund

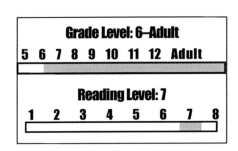

Grade Level: 6–Adult

5	6	7	8	9	10	11	12	Adult

Reading Level: 7

1	2	3	4	5	6	7	8

Number of Pages: 192

Copyright: 2001

Type of Publication:

Reproducible Teacher Book

J. WESTON WALCH
PUBLISHER

321 Valley Street
P.O. Box 658
Portland, Maine 04104-0658

To place orders: 1-800-341-6094
To fax orders: 207-772-3105

www.walch.com

With this sourcebook of reproducible puzzles, activities, and practice problems, you can successfully reinforce first-year algebra skills with all your students. Secret codes, magic squares, cross-number puzzles, and other self-correcting devices provide stimulating and fun practice. Chapters cover basic equations, equations and inequalities with real numbers, polynomials, factoring, fractions, graphing, systems of linear equations, and rational and irrational numbers. In addition, hands-on "outdoor math" activities have been added.

See your students build a better understanding of basic algebraic skills and concepts. With *80 Activities to Make Basic Algebra Easier* you get:

- Short, easy-to-understand activities that use a variety of instructional methods and may be used as a means of concept introduction and/or independent or group learning

- Material that is revised to address the NCTM standards, packed with teaching tips and up-to-date calculator activities

- Teacher support including background information, practical teaching suggestions, a complete answer key, and more

JWW0128

80 ACTIVITIES TO MAKE BASIC ALGEBRA EASIER
SAMPLE PAGES

TABLE OF CONTENTS

321 Valley Street
P.O. Box 658
Portland, Maine 04104-0658
207-772-2846

J. WESTON
WALCH
PUBLISHER

To place orders: 1-800-341-6094
To fax orders: 207-772-3105

www.walch.com

JWW0128

80 ACTIVITIES TO MAKE
BASIC ALGEBRA EASIER
SAMPLE PAGES

TABLE OF CONTENTS

321 Valley Street
P.O. Box 658
Portland, Maine 04104-0658
207-772-2846

J. WESTON
WALCH
PUBLISHER

To place orders: 1-800-341-6094
To fax orders: 207-772-3105

www.walch.com

JWW0128